How to Cook
Like a Southerner

HOW TO COOK LIKE A SOUTHERNER

Classic Recipes from the South's Best Down-Home Cooks

by

Johnnie Gabriel

with photography by STEPHANIE MULLINS

and food and prop styling by TERESA BLACKBURN

NELSON BOOKS

An Imprint of Thomas Nelson

Published in Nashville, Tennessee, by Nelson Books, an imprint of Thomas Nelson. Nelson Books and Thomas Nelson are registered trademarks of HarperCollins Christian Publishing, Inc.

Photography by Stephanie Mullins

Food and prop styling by Teresa Blackburn

Thomas Nelson, Inc., titles may be purchased in bulk for educational, business, fund-raising, or sales promotional use. For information, please e-mail SpecialMarkets@ThomasNelson.com.

Images on pages 24, 48, 64, 86, 140, 176 © photodisc
Image on page 2 © Shutterstock.com/Hitdelight
Image on page 69 © Shutterstock.com/Olga Pink
Image on page 83 © Shutterstock.com/phofotos
Image on page 84 © Fotolia
Image on page 133 © Shutterstock.com/Serenethos
Image on page 228 © Brebca—Fotolia
Image on page 230 © JJAVA—Fotolia
Image on page 234 © bit24—Fotolia

Library of Congress Cataloging-in-Publication Data

Gabriel, Johnnie, 1945–
  How to cook like a Southerner : classic recipes from the South's best down-home cooks / Johnnie Gabriel.
      pages cm
  Includes bibliographical references and index.
  ISBN 978-1-4016-0505-6 (alk. paper)
  1. Cooking, American—Southern style. I. Title.
  TX715.2.S68G333 2014
  641.5975—dc23   2013042877

Printed in the United States of America

14 15 16 17 18 QG 6 5 4 3 2 1

This book is dedicated to the special ladies in my life: my godly mother, Carol Heath Howell; my grandmothers, Mommee, Charlye Paul Heath, and Big Mama; Kate McClusky Howell; my Aunt LaNell Heath Merrill, who taught me to love wholeheartedly, live joyously, and work hard. Also, to my daughters: Stephanie Payne-Gabriel Bahm and Laura Payne-Gabriel, who gave me every reason to do so. And to Ed Gabriel, who has always supported me.

CONTENTS

FOREWORD

My cousin, Johnnie, and I grew up in the heart of the South, but y'all probably know that by now. We grew up in the heat of the Georgia sun, tugging on our Mamas' aprons, playing hard, and laughing even harder. We were raised with a passion for family, and stickin' with each other through thick and thin. But perhaps one of the best parts about growing up in the South is that we were brought up on some mighty fine recipes. And when I say, "mighty fine," I mean these were the brand of recipes that, as kids, we knew we wanted to hang on to for the rest of our lives. Our plates were always licked clean!

It's no wonder Johnnie and I both pursued careers cooking for other people—we come from a whole family of cooks! I remember Grandmother Paul teaching me her recipes in the kitchen. She didn't even need a recipe most of the time, because her hands worked from memory. And I know Johnnie has similar memories, too—we all do.

When most folks think about food in the South, they think of a few things: fried chicken, mac 'n cheese, and maybe some sawmill gravy thrown in for good measure. The truth is, though, that we have so much more to offer, and few can say it as well as my darlin' cousin. That's what this whole cookbook is about, sharing every delicious recipe and ingredient that the South has to offer. She's rounded up the finest recipes from all over, from friends and family alike to share. And I have to say, y'all, she didn't leave anything out. (I wouldn't trust anyone else to put this together, either. Heck, I only trust Johnnie to make wedding cakes for my family!)

As I thumbed through the pages of Johnnie's gorgeous *How to Cook Like a*

Southerner, I couldn't help but smile. The recipes on these pages will make you do that, y'all. Whether it's an old classic, like smothered steak or squash casserole, or a new favorite, like fresh roasted broccoli, I couldn't wait to get into my kitchen and whip something delicious up for Michael.

Want me to let you in on a little secret? You see, while the rest of the country is raving over this new "farm to table" fad, it's something we've been proud of doing our whole lives here in the South. Generation after generation of Southerners has eaten freshly grown vegetables from our families gardens. We still want those vegetables, but now most of us just have to purchase them rather than grow them ourselves. We love our vegetables, and we know just how to fix 'em so that everyone comes back for seconds.

One other thing I love about Johnnie's book is that she's really expanded the idea of what it means to be Southern; it's more than just the lower right-hand corner of the U. S. map. Our Southern palates have grown to appreciate recipes from all over the country, and we've somehow made them our own. She's included recipes for a breath-taking chicken piccata, a slap-yo'-mama good seafood gumbo from Mississippi, and a down-home shrimp and grits recipe from beautiful Southern Carolina. And did I mention the southwest chili?

So as you open up this book for yourself, know that Johnnie herself is opening up her home to you, and inviting you to come over and sit a spell. And when you're following along the recipes in this book, I hope that you're creating the same magical memories for your families, as Johnnie has for our family.

—PAULA DEEN

INTRODUCTION

When our long growing season begins, we once again enjoy the fresh fruits and vegetables that we cherish here in the South—peaches, butterbeans, peas, squash, tomatoes, cucumbers. With such an abundance of good food, how could we not have a tradition of delicious dishes!

I am so happy to come to you a third time with recipes using those fresh, tasty ingredients from Gabriel's Bakery and Restaurant, from family, and from friends. Many of these recipes have been passed down from generation to generation. I often have a customer eating in Gabriel's tell me, "This corn tastes just like my grandmother's." When customers speak of their families' traditional pound cakes or pie recipes, I can tell they are reminiscing about time well spent making memories.

There are traditions every family never wants to forget and recipes they cherish. When writing this book, I mentioned to Heather Skelton, my very patient editor, that the only recipes I have of my Grandmother Howell are in a black-and-white composition notebook that I put together for her when I was a child. The taste and look of her dishes are forever in my memory. She was an excellent cook and baker. The recipes are in her handwriting, my mother's, and mine. Some she cut from newspapers and taped to the pages. Most of the written recipes are ones neighbors shared with her. Unfortunately, the recipes her mother taught her to cook were only stored in her memory. She made scuppernong wine, pickles and preserves, and a strawberry cobbler that I can't recreate. The purpose of this third cookbook is to preserve these traditional recipes, expose you to some new ones, and introduce those of you who are unfamiliar with Southern cooking to some of our tried and true dishes.

I hope you cook, enjoy, and share these dishes with friends and family. Spending time in the kitchen with those you love can be a wonderful experience. My grandchildren have learned to enjoy time in the kitchen with their mom and dad and are truly proud when they put their dishes on the table. Many precious memories have been made there.

Along with traditional Southern dishes, you'll find in *How to Cook Like a Southerner* what I call some "new Southern" dishes. Several culinarily diverse regions make up the South, and basic ingredients and methods vary from one to another. For example, the southwestern region uses a few spices that a middle Georgia girl would not have had in the kitchen when growing up. Some recipes are not necessarily Southern but are just plain delicious. I am not a chef, but I believe I can recognize good food when I taste it. When good food from another region or culture is introduced to my palate, I attempt to adopt the flavors and spices into my culinary world. Every culture has its traditional dishes and for me all delicious, nutritious food is comfort food.

My time in the kitchen testing new recipes and reviving old family ones has been a great adventure. I bet you will enjoy them as much as I have.

P. S. I have noticed that a willing cook rarely lacks for friends or invitations!

How to Cook
Like a Southerner

BREAKFAST AND BRUNCH

Caramelized Onion and Goat Cheese Quiche

Gabriel's Grits

Brunch Egg Casserole

Egg Strata

Breakfast at Puddin' Place

Crab Quiche

Sausage Milk Gravy

Blueberry Muffins

Cranberry Coffee Cake

Country Ham and Red-Eye Gravy

Beignets

SOUTHERN CUISINE

Southerners have always loved their vegetables. We have such a long growing season here in the South there is usually an abundance of fresh food that can be pickled, canned, or frozen so we can enjoy our veggies in the winter. We are able to serve all year long one of our most popular meals at Gabriel's, our vegetable plate, cornbread or biscuit, and iced tea.

Of course, our traditional dishes are based on fruits and vegetables that are indigenous to our region as well as those that were introduced to this region from other continents. For instance, it was native Americans that convinced the early settlers that corn was worthy of eating. Without their knowledge of cultivating and catching of our natural resources, more of the early settlers would have starved than did. Hominy and grits, staples in a Southerner's diet, are made from corn. Seeds for collard greens, peas, okra, yams, watermelons, and the sesame seed were brought in from Africa. Latin Americans contributed limas, chocolate, white and sweet potatoes, and peppers.

In our early history wild game was abundant in the form of deer, rabbits, squirrels, birds, and ducks, as well as seafood along the coast, but the South's mild climate allowed for the cultivation of livestock and Southerners gravitated away from wild game. Pork, a staple meat in the Southern diet, was introduced by the Spanish when they brought herds of pigs on their expeditions.

Over the years, the amalgamation of foods and methods of cooking in the South has had delicious results, and Southern cuisine is still evolving. With changes in technology, the ability to procure foods from all regions with speed and preservation has expanded the Southern palate. The popularity of the Food Network and celebrity chefs like our own Paula Deen have helped to promote Southern cooking and introduce traditional dishes to other regions. Southern cuisine is both influencing and accepting of influence. Southerners love their food, and we have become very willing participants in the explosion of the culinary world.

CARAMELIZED ONION AND GOAT CHEESE QUICHE

Goat cheese is one of my favorite flavors. Put it in this quiche with caramelized onions and it's a winner! Not an onion lover? Swap out the onion for 3/4 cup halved, grape tomatoes.

1 (9-inch) deep-dish piecrust*
3 large yellow onions
3 tablespoons canola oil
Salt and black pepper to taste
1/8 teaspoon red cayenne pepper

5 large eggs
10 1/2 ounces whole milk
4 ounces goat cheese
1/8 teaspoon salt
Chopped fresh parsley for garnish

Preheat the oven to 350 degrees. Place the piecrust in the pie pan. Place aluminum foil over the cold piecrust and cover the foil with a layer of dried beans to keep the crust from puffing up during baking. Bake the piecrust for 20 minutes. Remove the beans and foil and prick the crust.

While the piecrust is baking, peel and slice the onions in uniform thickness. In a skillet, heat the canola oil over medium heat. Add the onions, stirring to coat, and sauté, initially stirring every 5 minutes until the onions start taking on a little color. Stir from the bottom every 2 to 3 minutes until the onions become a nice light golden color, but not dark and crisp. This can take 20 to 30 minutes if done properly, but will add a sweetness and enhance the flavor of the quiche. Once the onions are a nice golden brown, remove the pan from the heat and sprinkle the onions lightly with salt and pepper. Chop the onions, reserving 3/4 cup for the quiche filling. Season the reserved onions with cayenne pepper and refrigerate.**

Increase the oven temperature to 375 degrees.

In a large bowl whisk the eggs until they are blended. Whisk in the milk until it becomes a smooth mixture. Stir in the goat cheese, the 3/4 cup caramelized onions, and the salt. Carefully pour the mixture into the hot crust.

Bake for 30 to 35 minutes or until the edges are set and the center jiggles slightly. Let cool on a wire rack. Serve warm or at room temperature garnished with parsley.

Makes 6 servings.

* A store-bought piecrust can be used, but if time permits make a homemade crust. See recipe on page 193.
** Caramelized onions can be refrigerated for 3 to 4 days or frozen in an airtight container up to 3 months. They can be used in soups, vegetables, salads, dips, or meats.

GABRIEL'S GRITS

These grits are like candy to me. The only way I think they could be better is if I figured out how to make them chocolate flavored. We serve these at breakfast and with our shrimp as an entree.

....

2 1/4 level teaspoons salt
4 cups water

2 cups heavy cream
1 1/4 cups quick grits

....

Place the salt, water, and cream in a medium saucepan and bring to a boil over medium-high heat. Whisk in the grits. Turn the heat to medium-low and cook, whisking constantly, for 5 to 7 minutes. Enjoy!

Makes 4 1/4 to 4 1/2 cups.

Brunch Egg Casserole

My friend Sally Rhoden is one of the most generous, gregarious, and eager hostesses you will ever meet. I'm lucky to be invited often to meals she's prepared. Her family has its roots in Madison, Georgia. It doesn't get more Southern than that small, hospitable town. This recipe is in a family cookbook her daughter Jodi Rhoden put together when her brother married. Jodi is the author of Cake Ladies, *which features Southern stories and recipes. She is a talented young cake lady herself, with a precious cake shop in Asheville, North Carolina, called Short Street Cakes.*

2 cups classic-cut seasoned croutons
2 to 4 cups shredded sharp Cheddar
   cheese
4 large eggs, slightly beaten
2 cups milk
1/2 teaspoon salt

1/2 teaspoon prepared mustard
1/8 teaspoon onion powder
Dash of black pepper
4 slices bacon, cooked crisp and
   crumbled

Preheat the oven to 325 degrees. Grease a 1 1/2 quart (8 x 8-inch) casserole dish.

Place the croutons and cheese in the bottom of the casserole dish and combine. In a medium bowl combine the eggs, milk, salt, mustard, onion powder, and pepper. Mix until blended and pour over the crouton mixture. Sprinkle the bacon over the egg mixture and bake for 55 to 60 minutes, or until eggs are set.

Makes 6 servings.

NOTES: This dish can be assembled and refrigerated the day before baking. If you're serving a crowd, this recipe can easily be doubled. Just make sure you use a 9 x 13-inch dish.

PLAYING IN THE KITCHEN: Substitute half of the Cheddar cheese with Swiss cheese.

EGG STRATA

This is a recipe from my friend Sally Rhoden's family cookbook, Welcome Table. *It's a standard during Christmas at the Rhoden house.*

1 pound ground hot sausage
2 cups frozen hash browns
1 cup shredded Swiss cheese

6 to 8 large eggs, beaten
1/4 cup milk
Salt and black pepper to taste

Preheat the oven to 350 degrees. Spray a 9 x 13-inch casserole dish with a nonstick spray.

In a skillet over medium-high heat, add the sausage and brown. Remove the skillet from the heat and use a slotted spoon to remove the sausage. Drain well on paper towels. Transfer sausage to casserole dish.

Return the skillet to the heat and brown the hash browns in the sausage drippings, stirring occasionally to prevent burning. Layer the hash browns over the sausage. Top with the shredded cheese.

In a medium bowl stir the eggs, milk, salt, and pepper together and pour over the cheese, spearing with a fork at intervals to make sure the egg mixture soaks through.

Bake for 45 minutes.

Makes 6 to 8 servings.

Breakfast at Puddin' Place

Puddin' Place was the favorite place for the Rhoden family to stay in Oxford, Mississippi, when they visited their son Mitch attending the University of Mississippi. According to Emily Teddy, the mother of two young children, who tested this recipe for me, this is a good dish that children could help make. She says the children aren't the only ones who enjoyed eating them, though. She thought they tasted great and were quick, easy, and fun to make.

2 tablespoons butter, for greasing the baking dish
1/2 cup (1 stick) butter, melted
1 package large flaky layered refrigerator biscuits

Cinnamon sugar*
2 apples, peeled, cored, and sliced 1/4-inch thick

Preheat the oven to 350 degrees.

Butter the bottom and sides of a 9 x 13-inch casserole dish with 2 tablespoons of butter.

Separate the biscuits in 2 equal pieces horizontally. Dip the bottom halves in the melted butter, then in the cinnamon sugar. Place in the casserole dish in a single layer. Top the bottoms with an apple slice. Dip the biscuit tops in butter, then the cinnamon sugar, and place on top of the apple slices.

Bake for 20 to 30 minutes.

Makes 6 to 8 servings.

* You can purchase cinnamon sugar or make your own. To make homemade cinnamon sugar, mix 1/2 cup sugar with 1 tablespoon cinnamon.

CRAB QUICHE

Thanks to my friend Lynda Ausburn for this goodie.

2 (9-inch) deep-dish piecrusts*
1 tablespoon vegetable oil
1/2 cup green onions
1 1/2 cups half-and-half
3 large eggs

Salt and black pepper to taste
1/2 teaspoon dry mustard
1 1/2 cups canned backfin crabmeat
1 to 1 1/2 cups shredded Swiss cheese

Preheat the oven to 350 degrees.

Generously prick with a fork the bottoms of piecrusts so they prebake properly and bake them for about 10 minutes. Remove from the oven and let cool.

Preheat a small skillet over medium heat. Add the oil and the green onions and cook for up to 5 minutes. You just want to wilt the onions. Remove the skillet from the heat and allow the onions to cool a bit.

In a large bowl mix together the half-and-half, eggs, salt, pepper, and mustard.

Fold in the crab, cheese, and onions.

Pour the mixture into the piecrusts and cook for 45 minutes or until set.

Let cool for 10 to 15 minutes before cutting and serving.

Makes 12 to 16 servings.

* Store-bought piecrusts can be used, but if time permits make homemade crusts. See recipe on page xx.

SAUSAGE MILK GRAVY

*We serve this gravy with our fresh biscuits at Gabriel's. When you're looking for a hearty breakfast to start the day, this is it. The gravy can be made ahead and reheated.**

4 ounces pork sausage (we use a spicy, organic chicken sausage patty)
1/4 cup (1/2 stick) butter
1/3 to 1/2 cup all-purpose flour

3 cups whole milk
1/8 teaspoon red pepper flakes**
3 to 4 heavy pinches salt
1/2 teaspoon black pepper

In a medium skillet over medium heat, cook the sausage, breaking it up into small pieces with the back of a spoon. Continue to brown and break up the sausage until it is cooked through, about 5 minutes. Set the meat aside on a paper towel-lined plate to drain.

Add the butter to the skillet and allow to melt. Whisk in the flour and continue to cook and stir until the mixture is pale yellow, 2 to 3 minutes. Slowly whisk in the milk. Bring the mixture to a boil, whisking constantly until it becomes thick, about 10 minutes. Stir in the red pepper flakes, salt, and pepper. Add the sausage back to the skillet. Serve immediately.

Makes 2 to 3 cups, enough to serve 6 to 10 biscuits.

* If reheating, place the gravy in a heavy saucepan over very low heat. Microwave 1/2 to 3/4 cup milk until almost boiling and whisk into the gravy until it is thinned and pourable.
** I crush the pepper flakes as much as possible with a mortar and pestle.

Blueberry Muffins

These muffins are a breakfast and brunch favorite, and they are so easy to make.

1 1/2 cups all-purpose flour
1/2 cup sugar
2 teaspoons baking powder
1/2 teaspoon salt

1 large egg
1/2 cup milk
1/4 cup vegetable oil
1 cup fresh blueberries

Preheat the oven to 400 degrees. Grease 12 standard-size muffin tins or 24 mini muffin tins.

In a medium bowl combine the flour, sugar, baking powder, and salt, stirring to thoroughly distribute the ingredients.

Make a well in the center and add the egg, milk, and oil.

Stir until just combined.

Fold in the blueberries.

Distribute evenly among the muffin tins (about 3/4 full)and bake for 20 to 25 minutes. Cool briefly, then remove from the tins.

Makes 12 standard muffins or 24 mini muffins.

PLAYING IN THE KITCHEN: Add 1 cup of grated apple to the batter to add a little moisture and softened the texture a bit. A great way to sneak fiber into the diet.

CRANBERRY COFFEE CAKE

From my friend Emily Teddy's recipe collection, this coffee cake should be enjoyed with friends and a cup of good coffee.

Cake
1/2 cup (1 stick) butter, softened
1 cup sugar
2 large eggs
1 teaspoon almond extract
2 cups all-purpose flour, sifted
3/4 teaspoon baking soda
1 teaspoon baking powder
1/2 teaspoon salt
1 cup sour cream
1 cup chopped pecans
1 (14-ounce) can whole cranberry sauce

Topping
1 tablespoon butter, melted
1 cup powdered sugar
2 tablespoons warm water
1/2 teaspoon almond extract

Preheat the oven to 350 degrees. Grease and flour a 10-inch tube pan.

To make the cake: In a large bowl cream the butter and sugar with a stand mixer until fluffy. Beat in the eggs and almond extract.

In a medium bowl sift to combine the flour, baking soda, baking powder, and salt. Add to the egg mixture alternately with the sour cream. Add the chopped pecans.

Spread half of the batter into the tube pan. Spread the cranberry sauce over the batter. Top with the remaining batter.

Bake for 55 to 60 minutes or until lightly browned. Cool briefly, then remove from the pan.

To make the topping: In a small bowl whisk the butter, powdered sugar, water, and almond extract. Drizzle over the completely cooled cake.

Makes 12 to 14 servings.

COUNTRY HAM AND RED-EYE GRAVY

Have you ever received a country ham for a Christmas gift? Usually a real country ham comes in a cloth bag. Would you know how to cook it? My mother and grandmothers would have, but until I started asking friends and family for country ham recipes for this book, I can't say that I did. This recipe is a keeper. Serve it with eggs, spooned over grits, or with biscuits.

1 pound cured country ham, thinly
   sliced
1/2 cup milk
1 tablespoon vegetable oil

1/4 cup strong black coffee
1/4 cup water
1/8 teaspoon sugar

Place the sliced country ham and the milk in a large zip-top bag and let it sit overnight in the refrigerator to reduce the saltiness.

Remove the ham and wipe dry with paper towels.

Heat the oil in a skillet over medium heat.

Add the ham and cook briefly until the fat is cooked through and the ham has reached 160 degrees.*

Remove the ham from the skillet and set aside on a warmed plate.

Mix the coffee, water, and sugar together in a small bowl and pour into the pan.

Cook for 3 to 5 minutes over medium heat while stirring to dislodge any drippings from the bottom of the pan.

Makes 4 servings.

* I use a digital instant-read thermometer . . . worth the investment.

Beignets

These are a tradition for my friend Sally Rhoden's family. She loved them when she visited New Orleans, so she made sure her family and friends could enjoy them at home as well. In New Orleans, beignets are made with yeast and involve many steps. They are often served with café au lait, which is half strong coffee and half hot milk. You can easily make café au lait at home on a lazy Saturday morning while you're cooking this delicious quick version of beignets. What a special morning that will be!

Vegetable oil for frying
2 cups all-purpose flour
2 teaspoons baking powder
1/2 cup sugar
1 pinch salt

1 tablespoon melted butter
1 large egg, beaten
1 cup warm milk
Powdered sugar for serving

Pour the oil in a deep skillet to about 3 inches deep and heat on high until oil reaches 350 to 360 degrees on an instant-read thermometer.

Sift together the flour, baking powder, sugar, and salt into a medium bowl. Add the butter, egg, and milk. Blend together with a whisk. Let the batter sit at room temperature for 10 to 15 minutes before dropping by spoonfuls into the hot oil (temperature is very important) to fry. When golden brown on the bottom (this will happen quickly, about 3 minutes, if the oil is the right temperature), turn to brown on the other side. When golden on both sides, remove and drain well on a warm plate lined with paper towels. Sprinkle generously with powdered sugar and serve warm.

Makes 4 to 6 servings.

BREADS

Banana Bread

Easy Yeast Rolls

Cheese "Biscuits"

Cornbread

Cloister Cornbread

Emily's Three-Seeded Pan Rolls

Strawberry Tea Bread

Carrot Raisin Muffins with Honey Butter

Poppy Seed Bread

Buttermilk Biscuits

Zucchini Bread

Blueberry Muffins

Food and Fellowship

Along with spending time with my children and grandchildren and gardening, food and fellowship are the most important things to me. When I was in grammar school, my favorite place at the end of the day was under my dad's left arm as he sat propped up in his bed, reading chapters of the New Testament from his Bible. I would lay my head against his chest as he read until I fell asleep or he made me troop off to my own bed. My sister says I always wanted to be in a parent's or grandparent's lap or hang out with her and her friends. She is seven years older and found me terribly annoying and did not think this trait was very charming. Apparently not much has changed as I still enjoy the company of friends and family . . . but hopefully I'm not as annoying.

I am bountifully blessed with several groups of friends. The group with the longest history is my "Birthday Club," a group of ladies who attended the same church and originally shared a love of playing bridge. We eventually dropped the bridge, but always have dinner. We have experienced every major life event together, much joy and laughter, and from time to time, great sorrow. And oh, the food! Every month it seems we all want the hostess to share her recipes. From this group I have learned to appreciate really good food and fervent friendship.

Food has brought so many wonderful people into my professional life as well. We have cooked and baked together for customers and photo shoots, delivered wedding cakes together, tested recipes, and written, edited, and sold cookbooks. And it's all been done in the pursuit of good food with an added blessing of fellowship and friendship.

Bonds can and will be formed over a table of food that is prepared by hands that love us or love the preparation of food. What greater reward could we gain? My hope would be for everyone to find a common love and form this sort of bond with others over their lifetime.

Banana Bread

Jane Anne Countryman, a good friend and a member of my Sunday school class, often treats us to this bread. I don't know anyone who doesn't love this for breakfast, brunch, snack, or with an afternoon coffee or tea.

1/2 cup (1 stick) butter, softened
1 cup sugar
2 large eggs
3 ripe bananas, peeled and mashed

1 teaspoon vanilla extract
2 cups all-purpose flour
1 teaspoon baking soda
1 teaspoon salt

Preheat the oven to 350 degrees. Grease and flour a 9 x 5-inch loaf pan.

In a stand mixer fitted with the paddle attachment cream together the butter, sugar, and eggs. Add the bananas and vanilla and stir by hand until the bananas are evenly distributed.

In a small bowl sift together the flour, baking soda, and salt. Fold the flour mixture into the egg mixture and stir until just combined. Pour into the loaf pan and bake for 50 minutes. Cool briefly, then remove from the pan.

Makes 10 to 12 servings.

PLAYING IN THE KITCHEN: Toss about 1/2 cup of fresh blueberries with a little extra flour and shake off any excess. Fold into the wet mixture. Fold in 1/2 cup of pecans or walnuts after you've incorporated the flour mixture.

EASY YEAST ROLLS

Hot yeast rolls with butter are always delicious and comforting. This roll has more of a biscuit texture. It is so easy and requires no rolling. My friend Gail Schwartz shared this recipe with me. Spending time with her and experiencing her sweet spirit is just as comforting.

3 (.25-ounce) envelopes active dry yeast
1/2 cup warm water
5 cups self-rising flour
1 teaspoon baking soda

1 cup vegetable shortening
2 cups warm buttermilk, at room
  temperature*
2 tablespoons butter, melted

Dissolve the yeast in the warm water and set aside.

In a large bowl mix the flour and baking soda. With a pastry blender or two knives cut the shortening into the flour mixture until the shortening is evenly distributed and the pieces are no larger than a pea. Add the buttermilk and yeast and stir together until all of the flour is wet.

Grease two 12-cup muffin tins and one 6-cup muffin tin.

Flour your hands and form 1-inch balls of the dough. Place 3 balls into each cup of a muffin tin. Set in a warm spot for 15 to 20 minutes.

Preheat the oven to 350 degrees.

When ready to bake, brush the tops with melted butter.

Bake for 18 to 22 minutes. The rolls will be golden brown when done.

Makes 30 rolls.

* If you forget to take the buttermilk out of the refrigerator to let it come to room temperature, just heat it in the microwave straight from the refrigerator for two 30-second intervals at 60 percent power.

CHEESE "BISCUITS"

I don't remember my Big Mama, Grandmother Kate Howell, making these biscuits, but I found her handwritten recipe when I was doing the research for this cookbook. It seems to have been written in the fifties. This doesn't rise like a traditional Southern biscuit, and it's savory, containing the same ingredients as a cheese straw without the cayenne pepper. This little biscuit is really tasty as an appetizer or as an accompaniment to a green salad or a chicken or tuna salad.

1 cup all-purpose flour
1/4 teaspoon salt

8 ounces sharp Cheddar cheese, shredded
1/2 cup (1 stick) cold margarine, cubed

Combine the flour and salt in a large bowl. Add the cheese and margarine and cut into the flour with a pastry blender until the margarine is evenly distributed.

On a floured surface, roll the dough out to 1/4-inch thickness. Cut out biscuits with a 2-inch cutter and place on an ungreased cookie sheet about 1 inch apart.

These can be stored in the refrigerator overnight to bake later or baked as soon as they are rolled out.

When ready to bake, preheat the oven to 450 degrees. Bake for 7 to 8 minutes.

Makes 30 to 40 thin biscuits.

PLAYING IN THE KITCHEN: Cut in fresh rosemary or another fresh herb to the dough when you add the cheese and margarine.

Press a pecan half in the center of each biscuit.

Roll the dough 3/8-inch thick and form a little indentation in the biscuit with your thumb. Place 1/8 to 1/4 teaspoon of your favorite chutney* or jam in the indentation.

* The Cranberry Chutney on page 58 is delicious with these biscuits.

CORNBREAD

Cornbread is a Southern table staple. Growing up, we either had cornbread or biscuits at pretty much every meal except for breakfast. My grandparents Howell ate their biggest meal at lunch. Their evening meal, which they called supper, would sometimes consist of leftover cornbread and buttermilk or cornbread and pot liquor, which is what us Southerners call the seasoned liquid from a pot of cooked greens (see page 89). These days vegetable plates at Gabriel's hardly ever go out of the kitchen without a corn muffin. Cooking this in a cast-iron skillet will render a nice brown crust that is a signature of Southern cornbread.

4 tablespoons vegetable shortening or oil
1 2/3 cups white cornmeal
1/3 cup all-purpose flour
1 teaspoon salt

2 tablespoons sugar
1/2 teaspoon baking soda
1/2 teaspoon baking powder
1 1/2 cups buttermilk
1 extra-large egg

Preheat the oven to 450 degrees. Pour the shortening or oil into a 10- or 11-inch cast-iron skillet or 12-cup muffin tin and place in the oven for about 10 minutes. The oil should be really hot but not smoking.

In a large heatproof bowl combine the cornmeal, flour, salt, sugar, baking soda, and baking powder. Add the buttermilk and egg. Stir to combine and make a well in the center. Remove the hot pan from the oven and pour the hot oil into the well. Stir to combine and then pour the mixture into the cast-iron pan. You should hear it sizzle. If using muffin tins, fill each one three-fourths full. Bake for 15 to 18 minutes or 10 to 12 minutes if making corn sticks.

Cut into wedges in the pan or turn out onto a warm plate and serve hot with real butter and honey.

Makes 8 to 10 wedges, 12 muffins, or 16 corn sticks.

CLOISTER CORNBREAD

This recipe is from Judy Shuford, my friend Sally Rhoden's sister, who is also a great cook. The Cloister is a five-star resort at Sea Island, Georgia, just across a short bridge from St. Simons Island, Georgia. Word has it that this is their cornbread recipe. If we can't all stay at the Cloister, at least we can enjoy the cornbread!

3/4 cup (1 1/2 sticks) butter, softened
1/2 cup sugar
4 large eggs
4 ounces bacon, rendered* and diced
   (about 5 slices)
12 ounces cream-style corn

1 cup shredded Cheddar cheese
1 cup shredded Monterey Jack cheese
2 cups pastry flour**
1 1/4 cups yellow cornmeal
4 tablespoons baking powder
1 teaspoon salt

Preheat the oven to 350 degrees. Grease two 12-cup muffin tins.

In a large bowl cream the butter and sugar with a stand mixer until fluffy. Add the eggs one at a time, mixing between each addition. Add the bacon, corn, cheeses, pastry flour, cornmeal, baking powder, and salt. Mix until well incorporated.

Fill the muffin tins halfway and bake for 20 minutes.

Makes 20 to 24 muffins.

* Cook the bacon until the fat is released.
** To make pastry flour, combine 3 parts all-purpose flour with 1 part cake flour. For this recipe, mix 1 1/2 cups all-purpose flour and 1/2 cup cake flour.

EMILY'S THREE-SEEDED PAN ROLLS

These rolls are beautiful. They are great for a dinner party or to make sandwiches with leftover meat. Serve them hot out of the oven with roast beef and a horseradish spread or with leftover turkey and a cranberry aioli (see recipe on page 247). Add a roasted vegetable or side salad and fresh fruit.

2 tablespoons plus 1 teaspoon fennel seeds

2 tablespoons plus 1 teaspoon poppy seeds

2 tablespoons plus 1 teaspoon sesame seeds

12 frozen yeast bread dough rolls

2 large egg whites, beaten

1/4 cup (1/2 stick) butter, melted

Lightly spray a 10 x 10-inch baking pan with nonstick cooking spray.

Combine the fennel, poppy, and sesame seeds in a small bowl. Dip the dough rolls, one at a time, in the egg whites and then roll in the seed mixture.

Arrange the rolls, 1 inch apart, in the baking pan.* Spray a piece of plastic wrap with nonstick cooking spray and cover the rolls.

Let the rolls rise in a warm place for 2 to 4 hours until doubled in size.

Preheat the oven to 350 degrees. Uncover the rolls and bake for 15 minutes or until golden. Brush with melted butter and serve warm.

Makes 12 rolls.

* The rolls bake best and hold a good shape when placed 1 inch apart and almost fill the pan, leaving an inch from the roll to the side of the pan.

STRAWBERRY TEA BREAD

From the recipe collection of Emily Teddy, who helped me test and edit recipes for this book. What a good time we had.

2 (10-ounce) packages frozen
   strawberries, thawed and diced large
4 large eggs
2 cups sugar*
1 1/4 cup vegetable oil

3 cups all-purpose flour
1 teaspoon baking soda
1 teaspoon salt
3 teaspoons cinnamon
1 1/4 cups chopped pecans

Preheat the oven to 350 degrees. Grease three 8 x 4-inch loaf pans.

In a large bowl combine the strawberries, eggs, sugar, and oil.

In another large bowl combine the flour, baking soda, salt, and cinnamon. Add the strawberry mixture to the flour mixture and mix. Add the nuts and stir.

Pour into the loaf pans.

Bake for almost 50 minutes or until a cake tester** inserted into each loaf comes out clean. Cool briefly, then remove from the pan. Let cool and serve.

Makes 3 small loaves.

NOTE: This bread freezes well.

PLAYING IN THE KITCHEN: Cream cheese spread on top is a nice addition.

---

* If using sugared frozen strawberries, reduce to 1 cup.
** A cake tester (a thin metal probe) can be purchased inexpensively, sometimes in a grocery store. If you don't have one just use a long toothpick.

Carrot Raisin Muffins with Honey Butter

These little muffins are packed with lots of goodies! They contain plenty of fiber, spices, and honey butter. I can't think of a more flavorful way to begin the day. They would be a delicious, filling addition to a young one's lunch box or to have on hand for a healthy afternoon snack.

5 large eggs
1 1/4 cups vegetable oil
1 1/4 cups sugar
3 cups coarsely grated carrots
1 1/4 cups golden raisins
1 1/4 cups chopped walnuts, toasted
1 cup applesauce
1/2 cup shredded coconut

3 3/4 cups all-purpose flour
5 1/2 teaspoons baking powder
2/3 teaspoon salt
2 teaspoons ground cinnamon
2 1/2 teaspoons ground nutmeg
2 tablespoons honey, optional
2 tablespoons butter, softened, optional

Preheat the oven to 400 degrees.

Grease two 12-cup muffin tins or line with paper liners.

In a large bowl beat the eggs, oil, and sugar until smooth. Add the carrots, raisins, walnuts, applesauce, and coconut and stir just enough to combine.

In a medium bowl mix the flour, baking powder, salt, cinnamon, and nutmeg. Add to the carrot mixture and stir, combining well.

Scoop the batter into tins and bake for 18 to 20 minutes or until a tester* comes out clean.

If using butter and honey, melt the butter in the microwave and stir in the honey. Brush over the top of the muffins after removing them from the oven.

Makes 20 to 24 muffins.

** A cake tester (a thin metal probe) can be purchased inexpensively. If you don't have one just use a long toothpick.

POPPY SEED BREAD

This is such a classic and so is my friend Jean Moore, who shared this recipe with me. We've shared lots of good times and "life" times, and good food is usually a big part of them both. I know you'll make memories with those for whom you bake and share this well-loved bread.

Bread
3 cups all-purpose flour
1 1/2 teaspoons salt
1 1/2 cups milk
1 1/2 teaspoons baking powder
3 large eggs
1 1/2 teaspoons almond flavoring
2 1/2 cups sugar
1 1/2 teaspoons butter flavoring
1 1/8 cups canola oil
1 1/2 teaspoons vanilla flavoring
1 1/2 tablespoons poppy seeds

Glaze
1/2 teaspoon almond flavoring
1/2 teaspoon butter flavoring
1/2 teaspoon vanilla flavoring
1/4 cup orange juice

To make the bread: Preheat the oven to 350 degrees. Grease and flour three 8 1/2 x 4 1/2-inch loaf pans or 1 Bundt pan.

In a large bowl combine the flour, salt, milk, baking powder, eggs, almond flavoring, sugar, butter flavoring, canola oil, vanilla flavoring, and poppy seeds. Mix well.

Pour into the pan(s) and bake for 50 minutes in the loaf pans and 60 to 70 minutes in a Bundt pan. While the bread is baking, prepare the glaze.

To make the glaze: Combine the almond, butter, and vanilla flavorings in a small bowl and whisk in the orange juice. Allow to stand while the bread bakes. After removing bread from the oven, while the bread is still in the pan, pour the glaze over the bread and let set until cooled, 15 to 20 minutes.

Makes 3 loaves (8 to 10 servings each) or 1 Bundt pan (14 to 16 servings).

NOTE: This bread freezes well.

BUTTERMILK BISCUITS

A young friend of mine and mother of two, Stephanie Ausburn McGill, shared this recipe with me after her mom, Lynda Ausburn, commented that Stephanie made "the best biscuits she had ever eaten." Coming from Lynda, who is known in Marietta to be a good cook, I couldn't rest until Stephanie shared her secret with me.

2 cups self-rising flour
1/2 teaspoon kosher salt
1/4 cup (1/2 stick) cold butter, cut into
    pieces

1/4 cup cold vegetable shortening
3/4 to 1 cup buttermilk

Preheat the oven to 500 degrees.

Combine the flour and salt in a large bowl. Cut the butter and shortening into the flour with a pastry blender until the mixture resembles coarse crumbs (you want some pea-size pieces of butter to remain).

Pour about 3/4 cup buttermilk into the flour mixture and give a few stirs to determine how much more liquid to add. Don't stir too much—basically just turn the dough over with a spoon so that it begins to come together. I like the dough to be a little wet, but not too wet to cut out. As you experiment with this recipe, you will determine exactly how much buttermilk you will prefer to use based on the workability of the dough.

Turn the dough out onto well-floured parchment or waxed paper. Sprinkle enough flour on top so that the dough doesn't stick to your fingers. Pat down the dough to about 1-inch thickness. Turn the dough over and sprinkle a little flour on top. This will keep the dough from sticking as you continue to pat down and fold. Using the parchment paper, lift the dough and fold it in half. Sprinkle a little more flour on top, press down to 1 inch, and fold in half again. Repeat this process until you have folded it 4 times. Pat down to 1/2 inch and then use a 2- or 3-inch round cutter to cut out biscuits. Press the scraps together and cut out until all the dough is used.

Place the biscuits almost touching on a greased cast-iron skillet or cookie sheet. (For crispier biscuits place an inch apart.) Brush the tops with buttermilk. Bake for about 10 minutes or until the tops are starting to brown. Serve immediately.

Makes 8 to 12 biscuits, depending on the size of the biscuit cutter.

PLAYING IN THE KITCHEN:
Add 1 cup of grated apple to the
mixture to add a little moisture and
soften the texture a bit. A great way to
sneak fiber into the diet.

ZUCCHINI BREAD

I love squash almost any way you can cook it. This bread just gives me one more option. This is a must recipe for a backyard gardener with a bumper crop of zucchini. Stephanie Ausburn McGill's friend serves it to her guests at 100 Acre Farm, a bed and breakfast in Madison, Georgia.

3 large eggs
1 cup canola oil
2 cups sugar
1 1/2 teaspoons vanilla extract
2 1/2 cups shredded zucchini
1 (8-ounce) can crushed pineapple, drained

3 cups all-purpose flour
2 teaspoons baking soda
1 teaspoon salt
1/2 teaspoon baking powder
1 1/2 teaspoons ground cinnamon
3/4 teaspoon ground nutmeg

Preheat the oven to 350 degrees. Grease and flour two 8 x 4-inch loaf pans.

In a large bowl beat the eggs. Add the oil, sugar, and vanilla and beat until foamy. Stir in the zucchini and pineapple.

In medium bowl sift together the flour, baking soda, salt, baking powder, cinnamon, and nutmeg. Stir into the egg mixture.

Divide the batter equally among the pans and bake for 50 minutes. Cool briefly, then remove from the pan.

Makes 10 to 12 servings per loaf.

Zucchini Bread (page 43)

Fresh Apple Bread or Pound Cake

Many years ago friends Ann Veal and Joan Goddard both shared their recipes for fresh apple bread with me. It quickly became a favorite at my house. When I began baking professionally, this recipe quickly became a customer favorite as well.

Cake
1 cup sugar
1 cup vegetable oil
3 extra large or jumbo eggs
1 teaspoon vanilla
3 cups sifted all-purpose flour
1 teaspoon baking soda
1 teaspoon salt
1 teaspoon cinnamon
1 teaspoon nutmeg
1 teaspoon cloves

5 Granny Smith apples, peeled, cored, and diced small
1 cup chopped pecans

Glaze
1 cup light brown sugar
$1/2$ cup (1 stick) butter
2 tablespoons milk
$1/2$ teaspoon vanilla

To make the cake: Preheat the oven to 325 degrees. Spray a pound cake pan or a loaf pan with a nonstick spray. In the bowl of a stand mixer or in a large bowl combine the sugar, oil, eggs, and vanilla. Us the paddle attachment to beat at medium speed long enough to thoroughly combine, scraping down the bowl several times. In a medium bowl, sift together the flour, baking soda, salt, cinnamon, nutmeg, and cloves. Add the dry mixture to the egg mixture and mix at a medium speed just long enough to combine. Fold in the apples and pecans, distributing throughout. Pour the batter into the prepared pan. Tap the pan on countertop to settle the batter. Bake for 50 to 60 minutes or until a cake tester inserted into the center comes out with just a crumb or two.

To make the glaze: About 10 minutes before the cake is finished baking combine the brown sugar, butter, milk, and vanilla in a heavy duty saucepan. Bring to a boil and cook for 1 minute. Remove the cake from the oven and pour the hot glaze over the cake while it is still in the pan. Let cool in the pan for 10 to 15 minutes and turn out onto a serving plate.

Serves 12 to 14.

STARTERS AND SALADS

Sundried Tomato and Cheese Tureen

Avocado, Tomato, and Feta Cheese Salad

Parmesan Salad

Salad with Gorgonzola Cheese and Walnuts

Blue Cheese Wafers

Basic Vinaigrette

Spinach Salad Dressing

Texas Firecrackers

Brie and Cranberry Chutney Melt

Bacon, Lettuce, and Fried Green Tomato Sandwich

Hot Pimento Cheese Dip

SUNDRIED TOMATO AND CHEESE TUREEN

This colorful, elegant hors d'oeuvre comes from the Teddy–Marietta family of Marietta, Georgia, and Austin, Texas. This dish can be prepared a couple of days ahead and is so worth the planning and effort!

8 ounces cream cheese, softened
1 cup (2 sticks) butter, softened
12 ounces goat cheese
1 to 2 cloves garlic

8 ounces basil or sun-dried tomato pesto, refrigerated
8 ounces sun-dried tomatoes packed in oil
Few fresh basil leaves

Place the cream cheese, butter, goat cheese, and garlic in the bowl of a food processor. Blend until thoroughly mixed. Leave out to soften to spreading consistency.

Remove the pesto from the refrigerator and discard the oil layer off the top.

Drain the tomatoes, blot with paper towels, and chop.

Line a 1 1/2-quart bowl with a cheesecloth* folded twice. Place a few basil leaves in the bottom of the bowl to form a design on the top of the tureen when you invert the dish.

Divide the softened cheese mixture into fifths, about 4 ounces per layer. Spread one-fifth of the mixture on top of the basil leaves. Spread half of the pesto mixture on top of the cheese mixture. Cover with another layer of the cheese mixture and then half of the chopped sun-dried tomatoes. Spread another layer of the cheese mixture on top. Spread the other half of the pesto mixture on top, followed by another layer of cheese and the other half of the tomatoes. Finish with the cheese mixture.

Refrigerate until firm.

Remove from the refrigerator and invert onto a serving plate. Keep covered with the cheesecloth until ready to serve.

Serve with cut baguettes of French bread.

Makes 12 to 14 servings.

PLAYING IN THE KITCHEN: Jeanne Marietta of Texas, the Lone Star state, forms a star with the basil leaves. See how creative you can get.

* Cheesecloth is available in the grocery store sometimes with the cooking utensils, but you have to look hard.

AVOCADO, TOMATO, AND FETA CHEESE SALAD

I'm part of a group of single ladies here in Marietta who loves to get together for an evening of laughs and sharing. The food is always good and the company great. Carol Moore shared this appetizer with us.

2 avocadoes, peeled, pitted, and
  chopped
4 Roma tomatoes, chopped
1 small red onion, chopped
1 bunch fresh cilantro, trimmed and
  chopped

4 ounces feta cheese, crumbled
1/4 cup olive oil
1 tablespoon red wine vinegar
1 tablespoon ground cumin
1 teaspoon sea or kosher salt

In a medium bowl combine the avocadoes, tomatoes, and onion. Mix gently. Stir in the cilantro and feta. In a small bowl whisk the olive oil, red wine vinegar, cumin, and salt together and then pour over the avocado mixture. Mix well but gently. Cover and chill in the refrigerator.

Serve with blue corn chips, thin rice wafers, or thin crackers or over a bed of butter lettuce, with a colorful garnish of a green olive or a sliver of pimento. Refrigerate leftovers for up to 2 days.

Makes 8 servings as a salad or 20 as an appetizer.

Parmesan Salad

This fresh, crisp salad from my friend Jeanne Brown's Rhoden family cookbook has ingredients similar to my favorite Caesar salad. Add olives and bacon, two more ingredients that I'm partial to, and you've captured my attention. Thanks, Jeanne!

Dressing
1 clove garlic, minced
1/2 teaspoon salt
1/4 teaspoon black pepper
Pinch of dry mustard
2 tablespoons Parmesan cheese, grated
1 tablespoon lemon juice
1/4 cup vegetable or olive oil
Dash of Worcestershire sauce

Salad
1/4 cup black olives, sliced
1 head Bibb or iceberg lettuce, washed
   and torn
3 green onions, chopped
1/4 cup cooked bacon, crumbled

In a bowl or salad dressing bottle combine the garlic, salt, pepper, and mustard and mix well. Stir in the Parmesan cheese, lemon juice, oil, and Worcestershire. Refrigerate if not using in the next few hours.

In a large bowl, combine the olives, lettuce, green onions, and bacon on top. Cover and chill in the refrigerator until ready to serve. Add the dressing and toss just before serving.

Makes 6 servings.

SALAD WITH GORGONZOLA CHEESE AND WALNUTS

More good food from the table of Sally Rhoden. Just thinking about the distinct salty flavor of the Gorgonzola cheese, the tartness of the Granny Smith apple, and the crunch of the walnuts makes me want to sit down right now and enjoy this melody of flavors. Makes a great main dish for lunch or a side at dinner.

Dressing
1/2 cup olive oil
1/4 cup walnut oil
3 tablespoons balsamic vinegar
2 tablespoons sherry vinegar
Pinch of salt
Pinch of black pepper

Salad
1/2 cup walnuts, roughly chopped
1 large head romaine lettuce, washed
2 Granny Smith apples, cored and sliced
12 ounces gorgonzola cheese, crumbled

To make the dressing: Whisk the olive oil, walnut oil, balsamic vinegar, sherry vinegar, salt, and pepper together in a bowl. The dressing can be made up to 2 days before you plan to serve this salad. Store in the refrigerator.

To make the salad: Preheat the oven to 350 degrees. Place the walnuts on a cookie sheet and lightly toast for 5 to 7 minutes, stirring as needed to toast evenly. Watch carefully as nuts will quickly burn. Cool before adding to salad.

Tear the romaine into bite-size pieces, removing the large ribs if you don't care for them. Put the romaine, walnuts, apples, and cheese in a salad bowl and toss. Add dressing sparingly, according to your preference. Serve immediately.

Makes 6 servings.

PLAYING IN THE KITCHEN: Use red leaf lettuce to add some color.

BLUE CHEESE WAFERS

We could never quite get our blue cheese wafers right at Gabriel's. We tried several different versions but were never happy with either the flavor or the presentation. Then one day a front-of-the-house person took an order for a few dozen, not knowing we had taken them off the menu. Jeffry, our pastry chef, decided he could either get mad and make a fuss or just take the opportunity to perfect the recipe. Below is the result of his efforts. I think he got it right!

1/2 pound blue cheese
1/2 cup (1 stick) butter, softened
1/4 teaspoon cayenne pepper

1 1/3 cups all-purpose flour
3 tablespoons poppy seeds

Preheat the oven to 350 degrees.

Place the blue cheese and butter in a large bowl and blend well with a mixer. In a medium bowl sift the pepper and flour together. Add the poppy seeds and stir into the butter mixture. Spoon the mixture into a piping bag. Pipe 3-inch sticks 1 to 1 1/2 inches apart onto ungreased cookie sheets and cook for 10 minutes.

Makes 6 1/2 to 7 dozen 3-inch straws.

BASIC VINAIGRETTE

This recipe from my friend Sally Rhoden is a good one to have on hand. Personalize it by adding your own favorite fresh herbs.

1 1/2 teaspoons finely minced shallot or green onion
1 1/2 teaspoons Dijon mustard
1 1/2 teaspoons lemon juice

1 1/2 teaspoons white wine vinegar
1/4 teaspoon salt
1/2 cup olive oil
Freshly ground black pepper

In a small bowl stir together the shallots, mustard, lemon juice, vinegar, and salt. Whisk the oil into the shallot mixture, pouring in a thin, steady stream. Continue whisking until the mixture is thick. Season with black pepper to taste. Serve immediately or cover and store in the refrigerator for up to one week.

Shake, stir, or whisk well before serving.

Makes 1/2 cup.

Spinach Salad Dressing

This salad dressing comes from a great cook and is delicious over a spinach salad. Marilynn Paris, a friend of Sally Rhoden, shared this recipe with me.

1 small onion, grated or chopped
2/3 cup sugar
1 teaspoon salt
1 teaspoon black pepper

1 teaspoon celery seeds
1 tablespoon prepared mustard
1/3 cup cider vinegar
1 cup vegetable oil

Place the onions, sugar, salt, pepper, celery seeds, mustard, vinegar, and vegetable oil in the blender. Mix until well combined. Store in the refrigerator up to 1 week.

Makes 2 cups.

TEXAS FIRECRACKERS

Emily Teddy moved to Marietta, Georgia, from Austin, Texas, and brought one of her family's favorite recipes with her. This is one Mariettans have become accustomed to enjoying when Emily is invited to a gathering. These are delicious served with cream cheese covered in jalapeño jelly.

1 package ranch dressing mix (not ranch dip)
2 1/2 teaspoons crushed red pepper
1 teaspoon cayenne pepper

1 teaspoon black pepper
2 teaspoons garlic powder
1 cup vegetable oil
4 sleeves (1 box) saltine crackers

In a large bowl mix the dressing mix, red pepper, cayenne pepper, black pepper, garlic powder, and oil together. Add the crackers and toss well. Spread the crackers out in a single layer on a large ungreased cookie sheet or parchment paper. Let sit for 30 minutes or until the oil and spices are absorbed into the crackers. Store in an airtight container up to 1 week.

Makes 112 crackers.

BRIE AND CRANBERRY CHUTNEY MELT

Another family fave from Emily Teddy via friends in Austin, Texas. This chutney makes a yummy appetizer, but it is also delicious on its own for the Thanksgiving or Christmas meal. The fresh cranberries are so flavorful. Combined with the apples and celery, the texture is phenomenal.

1 (8-ounce) round brie
1/3 cup Cranberry Chutney (recipe follows)

4 bacon slices, cooked and crumbled
Your favorite crackers for serving

Trim the rind from the top of the brie round. Place the brie on a microwave-safe plate. Top with the chutney. Microwave on high for 1 minute. Sprinkle with the bacon. Serve with crackers.

Makes 6 to 8 appetizer servings.

Cranberry Chutney

2 cups fresh cranberries
2 cups sugar
3 tablespoons water
1 apple, chopped
2 celery ribs, chopped
1 tablespoon grated orange zest

1 cup fresh orange juice
1 cup golden raisins
1/2 teaspoon ground ginger
1/4 teaspoon ground cloves

In a medium saucepan over medium heat, add the cranberries, sugar, and water and bring to a boil. Cook for 5 minutes. Add the apple, celery, zest, juice, raisins, ginger, and cloves. Cook, stirring often, for 35 minutes.

Remove from the heat. Chill before serving, if desired. Store in the refrigerator for up to 3 weeks.

Makes 2 1/2 cups.

BACON, LETTUCE, AND FRIED GREEN TOMATO SANDWICH

I thought it would be fun to create a bacon, lettuce, and fried green tomato sandwich. The fried green tomato slices are also delicious served hot as a side dish.

12 slices bacon
Balsamic Aioli (recipe follows)
8 to 10 slices hot Fried Green Tomatoes
   (recipe on page 119)
8 slices sourdough bread, toasted on one
   side

4 ounces fresh mozzarella, drained,
   thinly sliced
3 Roma tomatoes, sliced
4 large lettuce leaves (romaine, butter,
   or bibb)
Salt and black pepper to taste

Fry the bacon in a large skillet over medium heat and cook the bacon until crisp. Drain the bacon on a paper towel–lined ovenproof plate and keep warm in the oven.

Spread all 8 untoasted sides of bread with balsamic aioli.

On 4 slices of the bread, layer 3 slices of bacon on each piece of bread.

Cover the bread with thinly sliced mozzarella, hot fried green tomatoes, Roma tomato slices, and lettuce. Add salt and pepper to taste. Top with the remaining 4 bread slices. Slice sandwiches in half and serve.

Makes 4 servings.

Balsamic Aioli

1/2 cup mayonnaise
2 tablespoons balsamic vinegar
1/2 teaspoon salt

1/2 teaspoon minced garlic
1 teaspoon julienned fresh basil

In a small bowl whisk together the mayonnaise, balsamic vinegar, salt, minced garlic, and basil. Refrigerate until ready to serve or up to 3 days.

Makes 1/2 to 3/4 cup.

HOT PIMENTO CHEESE DIP

My mother's and grandmother's recipe for pimento cheese is the one we serve and sell at Gabriel's by the sandwich and by the pound, day in and day out. Our customers love it! I really wanted a warm appetizer using our pimento cheese, and here's the result. This is especially good with pita chips.

3/4 cup mayonnaise
1 teaspoon sugar
2 cups (8 ounces) shredded mild
   Cheddar cheese*
1 (2-ounce) jar diced pimentos, well
   drained

6 to 8 slices bacon, cooked crisp and
   chopped
1 to 2 Roma tomatoes, peeled and
   chopped
Pita chips for serving

In a medium bowl whisk the mayonnaise and the sugar. Add the cheese and the pimento, combining well.

Preheat the oven broiler on low setting.

Spread the desired amount of pimento cheese $1/2$ to $3/4$ inch deep onto an ovenproof serving plate. Sprinkle chopped bacon and tomato to taste over the top of the pimento cheese and place under the broiler until the mixture is hot and beginning to bubble. Serve hot with pita chips.

Makes 2 to 2 1/2 cups.

PLAYING IN THE KITCHEN: Substitute chopped Caramelized Nuts (recipe on
   page 251) for the bacon and tomato.

* Grate your own cheese; pre-shredded cheese will change the taste and consistency.

SOUPS AND STEWS

Beef Stew

Mushroom Soup

Ski Slope Soup

Sally's Famous Vegetable Beef Soup

Chili Blanco

Chicken and Dumplings

Meredith Dykes Brunswick Stew

Texas Chili

Basic Homemade Stock

Corn Chowder

BEEF STEW

My dad was a meat and potatoes guy, and my mom's beef stew was one of his favorite dishes. With hot biscuits, a green vegetable, and a piece of my grandmother's pound cake, he left the table a happy man. We had a family meal every night of the week.

4 large yellow onions
10 tablespoons vegetable shortening, divided
1 (28-ounce) can diced tomatoes, undrained
1 to 2 cups all-purpose flour
2 tablespoons salt
1/2 teaspoon pepper
2 1/2 pounds beef stew meat

3 cloves garlic, minced
4 cups boiling water
1 teaspoon Worcestershire sauce
7 to 8 carrots, peeled and cut into 2-inch pieces (about 3 cups)
Salt and black pepper to taste
4 to 5 Irish potatoes, peeled and cut into 3/4- to 1-inch cubes
2 cups frozen green peas

Peel and slice the onions vertically in half (from root to tip), then into fourths and continue until you have 16 wedges from each onion.

Caramelize the onions: melt 4 tablespoons of the shortening in a large skillet over medium heat. Add the onions, separating them and stirring. Turn the heat to low and cook until the onions begin to first clear and then take on some color, about 45 to 50 minutes. Set aside.

Place the tomatoes in a small saucepan and cook over low heat, simmering for 15 to 20 minutes, and set aside.

Combine the flour, salt, and pepper in a zip-top bag. Add the meat to the flour mixture and shake to coat the meat well.

Melt the remaining 6 tablespoons of shortening in a large Dutch oven over medium heat. Add the meat and brown, turning to brown all sides.

Add the garlic, boiling water, cooked tomatoes, and Worcestershire and stir to combine.

Bring to a simmer over medium heat. Once it begins to simmer, turn the heat to low, cover, and stir occasionally for 2 to 2 1/2 hours until the meat is tender.

Add 3 cups of the caramelized onions and the carrots. Simmer uncovered for another 10 minutes. Taste and add salt and pepper if needed. Add the potatoes and cook for another 25 to 30 minutes. Add the peas and cook for 15 more minutes. Serve with cheese biscuits (recipe on page 31).

Makes 12 servings.

NOTE: Any leftover caramelized onions can be stored in the refrigerator for several days and added to other dishes, such as the country fried steak (page 160).

PLAYING IN THE KITCHEN: Add fresh sliced mushrooms during the last 30 minutes of cooking time.

CLEANING MUSHROOMS

My assignment was to write a sidebar (publishing lingo) on cleaning mushrooms. *Well*, I thought, *that's easy. I've cleaned mushrooms for years*. However, after doing a little research, I realized there's great deliberation out there about the best method.

To begin with, when you are choosing your package of 'shrooms, pick the ones that look the cleanest and have the least debris in the package.

Here are four methods that you can experiment with for all types of mushrooms except for morels, which should always be washed with water:

1. Peel the mushroom with a sharp paring knife, starting under one edge of the mushroom and "peeling" off the top layer. Do this all around the top of the mushroom. Shake it good to be sure there is no debris underside in the gills and trim off the bottom of the stem.

   I had a chef explain to me that this was the best way to clean mushrooms. Due to the porous nature of the plant, he believed that washing cause them to absorb water and lose flavor. I have tried this method a few times, but it was just too time consuming for me.

2. Brush mushrooms with a soft brush, dusting the debris off the top and the underside of the gills. Trim off the bottom of the stem.

3. Using a damp paper towel, wipe off the tops and check the underside gills for debris. Trim off the bottom of the stem.

4. Put the mushrooms into a colander and spray them with a light shower, shaking them around to wash off the tops and the underside. Shake off excess water and lay out on paper towels to dry. A little bit of water is absorbed but not enough to change the flavor a great deal. If you're sautéing the mushrooms, that water will be cooked out anyway.

I'll play it by ear and use whichever method works best based on the amount of debris I find once I've opened the package and on whether I'm using them raw, in which case some loss of flavor might be detected, or cooking them, when any loss of flavor would probably go unnoticed.

Mushroom Soup

Several years ago my friend Dorothy Woodruff invited me over to dinner and served this soup. It was so fabulous I didn't forget it. Your family and guests will think this took you hours to make.

1 pound assorted mushrooms
6 tablespoons butter
2 cups finely chopped onion
1/4 cup all-purpose flour
1 cup water

1 3/4 cups chicken broth, plus more as needed
1 cup dry vermouth
1/2 teaspoon salt
1/4 teaspoon black pepper

Wipe off the mushrooms, slice, and then cut the slices in half vertically. In a deep skillet over medium heat add the butter and onions and sauté onions until translucent. Add the mushrooms and cook for 5 minutes, stirring often. Stir in the flour and cook for 2 minutes, stirring constantly. Stir in the water, broth, vermouth, salt, and pepper. Bring to a boil over medium heat, reduce the heat to low, and simmer uncovered for a couple of hours. If the soup gets too thick, dilute it with a little chicken broth.

Makes 8 servings.

Ski Slope Soup

My friend Gail Re shared this recipe with me. She has three beautiful daughters who all love to spend time together. This hearty soup is a result of their cooking endeavors. There is a bit of prep with the dicing and slicing, but it is well worth the effort to have in the freezer on a winter evening after all those carpools. If it's too thick when you reheat it, add a little full-bodied beer.

1 pound hot pork sausage
1 pound mild pork sausage
1 (15-ounce) can kidney beans, undrained
2 (28-ounce) cans diced tomatoes
1 (14.5-ounce) can diced tomatoes
1 green bell pepper, diced
1 quart water
2 teaspoons seasoned salt

4 large Yukon gold potatoes, unpeeled and cubed
1 teaspoon dried thyme
1 large onion, diced
2 bay leaves
2 to 3 cups cooked roughly chopped chicken
1 (15-ounce) can tomato sauce
3 1/2 to 4 cups chicken broth

In an 8-quart stockpot over medium heat, brown the sausages, breaking into small pieces with a wooden spoon. Pour off the fat and add undrained kidney beans, tomatoes, green pepper, water, seasoned salt, potatoes, thyme, onion, bay leaves, diced chicken, tomato sauce, and chicken broth. Bring to boil over medium heat, turn the heat to low, and simmer uncovered for 1 1/2 hours. You may need to add a little water if too thick. Remove the bay leaves. Serve with crusty bread. Store leftovers in the refrigerator for 3 to 4 days or freeze in airtight containers for 4 to 6 weeks.

Makes 12 servings.

SALLY'S FAMOUS VEGETABLE BEEF SOUP

The way my friend Sally Rhoden makes her vegetable soup is the way most folks did when I was a kid, using leftover vegetables, roast, and juices from cooking meats that had been stored in the freezer. After making a few pots of your own, you'll have your style and flavor profile you and your family like. I like to serve this vegetable soup with hot corn muffins.

1 beef soup bone
1 to 2 pounds stew meat
2 1/2 to 3 quarts water
Salt and black pepper to taste
Leftover roast, chopped into 1/2-inch chunks or shredded to bite size
Leftover vegetables such as green beans, carrots, corn, and butter beans (or a bag of frozen mixed vegetables)

2 to 3 potatoes, peeled and cut into 1/2-inch chunks
1 large yellow onion, diced
3 to 4 (14.5-ounce) cans diced tomatoes
1 (8-ounce) can tomato sauce
Beef bouillon granules or leftover pan juices as needed

In a large stockpot over medium-high heat bring the beef bone, stew meat, and water to a boil. Turn the heat to low, cover, and simmer for a couple of hours. Remove the soup bone. Add salt and pepper to taste, roast, vegetables, potatoes, onions, tomatoes, and tomato sauce.

Bring to a boil over medium heat, turn the heat down to low, and simmer uncovered for several hours. Watch to be sure you don't boil out all the liquid. If the liquid cooks out, make some broth from hot water mixed with beef bouillon granules and add to the pot. Simmer uncovered for another 15 minutes to allow the flavors to combine.

Makes 10 to 12 servings.

NOTE: Freeze leftovers in airtight containers and keep in the freezer for up to 2 months.

CHILI BLANCO

This tasty white chicken chili is from Cynthia Marietta, a late aunt of Emily Teddy, one of my cooking and testing buddies for this cookbook. After spending time with Emily I can tell that her family shared lots of good food and good times in Austin, Texas. Now she's sharing Cynthia's delicious chili recipe with us for all to enjoy.

1 pound (2 cups) dried Great Northern white beans, sorted and soaked in water overnight
10 cups chicken broth
2 garlic cloves, minced
2 medium onions, chopped and divided
1 tablespoon vegetable oil
2 (4-ounce) cans chopped green chilies
1 (28-ounce) can diced or quartered tomatoes, undrained

2 teaspoons ground cumin
1 1/2 teaspoons dried oregano
1/4 teaspoon ground cloves
1/4 teaspoon cayenne pepper
4 cups cooked chicken, diced
Salt to taste
Shredded Monterey Jack cheese for garnish
Chopped green onions for garnish

Combine the beans, chicken broth, garlic, and half of the onions in a large pot and bring to a boil over medium heat. Reduce the heat to low and simmer uncovered until the beans are very soft, about 2 hours, or until done. Add more broth if necessary.

In a skillet over medium heat sauté the remaining onions in oil until tender.

Add the chilies, tomatoes and juice, cumin, oregano, cloves, and cayenne pepper. Mix thoroughly and add to the bean mixture.

Add the chicken, cover, and continue to simmer over low heat for 1 hour. Taste and add salt as needed.

Garnish with the cheese and onions.

Makes 10 to 12 servings.

CHICKEN AND DUMPLINGS

Just like my Grandmother Howells'! If you wish, you can cook the chicken, making the stock, the day before you make the dumplings. Store the stock in the refrigerator overnight and skim any fat that might accumulate off the top and discard before you make the dumplings.

Soup
1 large (4- to 5-pound) fryer chicken,
   neck and gizzards removed
1 large onion, peeled and cut in half
3 to 4 carrots, peeled and cut into 4-inch
   pieces
3 to 4 stalks celery with leaves, cut into
   4-inch pieces
2 teaspoons salt
1/2 teaspoon black pepper

Dumplings
3 cups cake flour, plus more for flouring
   the board
3/4 teaspoon baking soda
1 teaspoon salt
1/2 teaspoon white pepper
4 1/2 tablespoons vegetable shortening
1 to 1 1/4 cups whole milk

To make the soup: In at least an 8-quart stockpot place the chicken, onions, carrots, celery, salt, and pepper. Cover with water plus a couple of inches. Bring to a boil over medium heat. Reduce the heat to low and simmer uncovered for about 1 hour or until the chicken is cooked through. The chicken is done when a thermometer inserted into the breast reads 165 degrees and into the thigh reads 175 degrees. The legs will be very loose and moveable.

To make the dumplings: After the chicken has been cooking for 30 minutes, begin making the dumplings. In a medium bowl mix the flour, baking soda, salt, and white pepper. Cut the shortening into the flour mixture with your fingertips until it looks like small peas. Add the milk in 1/4-cup increments, stirring with a spoon until a ball of dough begins to form. Do not overmix.

Spread additional flour out on a cutting surface and move the dough to the surface to bring the ball together. Coat a rolling pin with flour and alternately roll the dough vertically, then horizontally until it is 1/8 to 1/4 inch thick. You may need to coat the rolling pin with more flour several times to keep it from sticking to the dough.

Using a sharp knife, cut the dough into 1 x 3-inch strips. Lightly dust the strips with a little more flour, cover with plastic wrap, and set aside to let them season a bit while the chicken finishes.*

When the chicken is done, carefully remove it from the broth and set aside to cool. Retain any drippings or gelatin that accumulates while the chicken is cooling to add back to the broth. Remove the pot from the heat and allow to cool. When the chicken is cool enough to handle, pull the chicken from the bones, discarding the skin and bones. Shred the chicken into bite-size pieces. You will have 4 to 6 cups of chicken.

Pour the broth through a fine-mesh strainer lined with cheesecloth. Coffee filters or a paper towel will work also; it will just drain slower. Discard the vegetables. Pour 8 to 10 cups of broth back into the stockpot to cook the dumplings. Refrigerate or freeze any leftover for future use.

Bring the broth to a gentle simmer over low heat. Check the seasoning and add salt and pepper as needed. (I add about $3/4$ teaspoon salt and $1/8$ teaspoon of pepper.) Once the water is gently boiling, drop the dumplings in one at a time. Bring back to a gentle boil, cover, and cook for 6 to 8 minutes, gently stirring occasionally to make sure the dumplings are submerged. Reduce the heat to low and add at least 4 cups of the pulled chicken. Be sure there is plenty of broth to cover the chicken and dumplings as the mixture will continue to thicken.

Cook uncovered for 15 to 20 minutes more, being careful to just cook until the chicken is reheated and the dumplings are cooked through and don't taste doughy. Don't overcook the dumplings or they will fall apart.

Makes 6 to 8 servings.

* Once cut, the strips can be frozen for future use, but not refrigerated. It's important that the strips have a light dusting of flour to keep them from sticking together.

MEREDITH DYKES BRUNSWICK STEW

At Gabriel's we double this recipe. It's great for serving a large crowd or if you want to freeze some for later.

1/2 cup (1 stick) butter

3 cups chopped cooked chicken

3 cups chopped Idaho potatoes
(approximately 2 large)

2 cups (1/2 pound) chopped smoked pork
(we use 1/2 shredded pork and 1/2
honey smoked boneless ham)

1 cup chopped onion

1 quart homemade chicken stock or 1
(32-ounce) carton chicken broth

2 (14.5-ounce) cans stewed tomatoes,
undrained

1 (16-ounce) can lima beans, drained

1 (17-ounce) can cream-style corn

1 (8-ounce) can English peas, drained

1/4 cup liquid smoke

1 1/2 cups barbecue sauce (see recipe on
page 249)

Melt the butter in a large stockpot over low heat. Stir in the chicken, potatoes, smoked pork and/or ham, onion, and chicken broth. Bring to a boil, reduce the heat to low, and simmer, uncovered, for 20 minutes. Stir often to keep the mixture from scorching.

Add the tomatoes, limas, corn, peas, liquid smoke, and barbecue sauce.

Bring the mixture to a boil over medium-low heat. Reduce the heat to low and allow to barely simmer, uncovered, for 2 hours, stirring often.

Makes 8 to 10 servings.

TEXAS CHILI

Football tailgating and Super Bowl parties are the perfect times to stir up a pot of chili. In the South when the slightest hint of snow or ice is in the forecast, grocery stores experience a run on ingredients for chili and vegetable soup. In my research of chili recipes, I heard rumors that my ophthalmologist, Howard Borger, and his wife, Lori, had a Texas Chili Cook-Off winning recipe from his medical school days in Texas. This recipe has become a family favorite over the years. While the original recipe has been lost, the following is their favorite adaption. When testing this recipe I found the Borgers' version a bit too spicy for my taste, but I wanted to give you the opportunity to experience a true Texas chili.

1 1/2 small red onions, chopped
2 green bell peppers, chopped
1 large jalapeno pepper, seeded and
   chopped
2 to 3 pounds ground sirloin*(I used
   ground round)
4 (12-ounce) cans beer, divided
8 tablespoons good-quality chili powder

1 tablespoon chipotle chili powder
1 tablespoon ancho chili powder
2 tablespoons cumin
3 teaspoons salt
3 cloves garlic, chopped
2 (15-ounce) cans pinto beans,
   undrained

In a 6-quart stockpot over medium to medium-high heat, combine the onions, peppers, jalapeños, ground meat, and 1 1/2 cans of beer. Stir with a wooden spoon to break up the meat and cook, continuing to stir until all the meat is no longer pink. Reduce the heat to low, maintaining a simmer, and cook uncovered for about 45 minutes. Remove the pot from the stove and drain* off all the liquid.

Return the pot to the stovetop and add the chili powder, chipotle chili powder, ancho chili powder, cumin, salt, garlic, and 2 cans of beer. Bring to a boil and simmer over low heat for an hour or more. Add the pinto beans and cook long enough to heat the beans through. The Borgers suggest sometimes serving over white rice.

Makes 4 quarts.

PLAYING IN THE KITCHEN: Being the Georgia girl that I am, I added a
   28-ounce can of diced tomatoes, undrained, and 2 cans of black beans,
   drained, when I add the spices. I love tomatoes in my chili, so the 2nd time
   I cooked the Borgers' recipe, I added them along with black beans, another
   favorite of mine.

Basic Homemade Stock

Homemade stocks result in a much better final dish. You'll get a superior, richer flavor at a lesser cost. Stocks can be refrigerated for up to five days or frozen for a couple of months. Save any leftover pan juices from cooked meat or freeze them until you're ready to make stock.

4 quarts cold water
2 medium onions, quartered
2 cloves garlic, quartered

2 stalks celery, chopped in large pieces
2 carrots, peeled and cut in large pieces
2 bay leaves

In a large stockpot or saucepan over high heat, combine the water, onions, garlic, celery, carrots, and bay leaves. Bring to a boil, then reduce the heat to medium-low, cover partially, and simmer for at least 4 hours. Add additional water as necessary to maintain 2 quarts liquid.

Remove from the heat and strain through cheesecloth or a fine sieve into a storage container. Let cool before refrigerating or freezing.

Makes 7 to 8 cups.

CHICKEN STOCK: Add 3 pounds backs, necks, and/or bones from chicken.

BEEF STOCK: Add 1 1/2 pounds beef shank or other beef bones.

SHELLFISH STOCK: Add 1 1/2 pounds rinsed shrimp heads and/or shells.

Corn Chowder

My friend Lynda Ausburn makes this hearty chowder every winter. It makes a lot, so prepare to freeze half for later.

2 cups chopped bacon, plus a couple pieces for garnish
1/4 cup olive oil
6 cups chopped yellow onions (4 large onions)
1/4 cup (1/2 stick) butter
1/2 cup plus 2 tablespoons all-purpose flour
1 teaspoon salt
1 teaspoon black pepper

12 cups chicken broth
2 pounds white boiling potatoes, unpeeled and diced
10 cups (about 10 ears) fresh corn kernels, blanched,* or 3 pounds frozen
2 cups half-and-half
1/2 pound sharp white Cheddar cheese, shredded
3 to 4 green onions, sliced, for garnish

In a large stockpot over medium-high heat, cook the bacon in olive oil until the bacon is crisp, about 5 minutes. Remove the bacon with a slotted spoon and drain on paper towels.

Remove all but 2 tablespoons of the bacon grease and reduce the heat to medium. Add the onions and butter, cooking the onions until transparent, about 10 minutes.

Stir in the flour, salt, and pepper and cook for 3 minutes. Add the chicken broth and potatoes, bring to a boil, and simmer uncovered for 15 minutes, until the potatoes are tender.

Crumble the bacon and add to the soup along with the corn, then add the half-and-half and Cheddar. Cook for 5 more minutes, until the cheese melts. Season to taste with salt and pepper. Serve hot with a garnish of bacon and sliced green onions.

Makes 10 to 12 servings.

A NOTE FROM LYNDA: "I like to use a mixture of 1 pound frozen yellow sweet corn, 1 pound frozen creamed corn (reduce the amount of half-and-half to 1 cup), and 1 pound frozen shoepeg corn."

* Cut the kernels off the cobs and blanch in boiling water for 3 minutes. Drain before adding to the pan.

BOILING POTATOES

Boiling potatoes are sometimes called waxy potatoes, with a thin, smooth skin that can be long or round in shape. Their waxy flesh is low in starch but relatively high in sugar and moisture.

Because they tend to hold their shape when cooked, they work well in soups, casseroles, salads, and for roasting. When mashed, they become thick and lumpy instead of creamy.

Look for one of these varieties at your local grocery store: Round White, Round Red, Yellow Potato, Red Potato, Salad Potato, La Soda, Red La Rouge, Red Pontiac, Red Nordland, Red Bliss, Yellow Finnish, Ruby Crescent, and Australian Crescent.

SIDES

Collard Greens

Sweet Potato Casserole

Corn Casserole

Fried Corn

Fried Okra

Roasted Broccoli

Heavenly Potatoes

Warm Sweet Potato Salad

Pink-Eyed Peas

Squash Casserole

Coke and Cherry Congealed Salad

Orange Congealed Salad

Lime Congealed Salad

Field Peas with Snaps

Fried Green Tomatoes

Three-Bean Bake

Cornbread Dressing

Pinto Beans

Deviled Eggs

Cole Slaw

Macaroni and Cheese

Dinner Jacket Potato Salad

COLLARD GREENS

At Gabriel's we cook collards every other day, alternating with turnip greens. Growing up I always preferred turnip greens, but I've learned to love collards after eating them the way our chefs prepare them. Collards can be more bitter than turnips, calling for a bit of sugar to be added.

2 (2 to 2 1/2 pounds each) bunches of collards (or the equivalent of 4 to 5 quarts prewashed, packaged bags)
4 ounces bacon, about 6 to 8 pieces
1/2 large yellow onion
1/3 cup sugar

1/2 cup white or cider vinegar
2 teaspoons salt
3/4 teaspoon black pepper
3/4 to 1 cup chicken stock
6 cups water
Salt and black pepper to taste

If you're working with collard bunches, use a sharp knife to cut the stems off just where they begin to be really "leafy." Throw the stems away or add to your compost pile.

Then fill the sink with cold water and swish the collards around to remove any debris. If the collards are really gritty, you may need to put them through an additional washing.

Next, remove the center stem. It's personal preference as to how much stem you leave on the leaf and cook. I fold the leaves in half and strip the center stem completely. Some people like stems left as they supply even more fiber to the diet.

You can chop the collards at this point or cook the whole leaf and chop just before serving.

Sauté the bacon in an 8-quart stockpot over medium heat, lowering the heat if necessary to keep from burning. Remove the bacon when it's crispy, leaving the drippings, and drain bacon on paper towels. Add the onions and cook until they are translucent. Be careful not to let the bacon drippings burn. Chop the bacon. Return the bacon to the pot and add the sugar, vinegar, salt, pepper, chicken stock, and water, stirring to combine. Add the collards and increase the heat to medium-high. Bring to a low boil, lower the heat, and simmer uncovered about 1 1/2 hours. Initially, the collards will float to the top, so occasionally push them down into the water. If the liquid cooks out quickly, add more water and/or stock to keep the collards covered with liquid. You want to end up with pot liquor, the liquid the greens are cooked in.

Taste for tenderness and flavor and adjust the salt and pepper seasonings to your preference.

When ready to serve, using two sharp knives, chop the collards a bit, breaking the big leaves up into bite-size pieces.

Makes 8 to 10 servings.

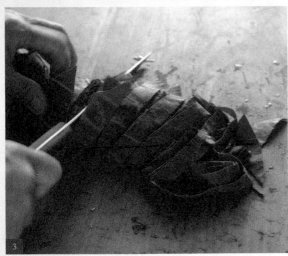

Hungry yet?

SWEET POTATO CASSEROLE

My friend Lynda Ausburn's family doesn't sit down to a holiday meal without her Aunt Fran's casserole. Every Southern family has their favorite version, but this one is different and flavorful because it's topped with crushed cornflakes as well as pecans and brown sugar. Using freshly baked sweet potatoes does make a superior dish.

3 cups baked and mashed sweet
   potatoes
3/4 cup sugar
2 large eggs
1/3 cup butter, softened
1 cup milk

3 teaspoons vanilla extract
1/2 cup light brown sugar
1/2 cup chopped pecans
3/4 cup crushed corn flakes
1/3 cup margarine, melted

Preheat the oven to 400 degrees. Grease a 9 x 13-inch casserole dish.

In a large bowl use a hand mixer to beat the potatoes, sugar, eggs, butter, milk, and vanilla together. Pour into the casserole dish. Bake for 20 to 30 minutes or until the mixture is hot and bubbling.

While casserole is cooking, combine the brown sugar, pecans, corn flakes, and melted margarine in a medium bowl and mix well.

Remove the casserole from the oven and add the topping mixture. Return to the oven for 10 more minutes.

Makes 10 servings.

Sweet Potato Casserole (page 93)

CORN CASSEROLE

Fresh corn cut straight from the cob is what makes this dish extra special and full of flavor. I have a memory of helping my mother and grandmothers shuck corn so that we could freeze it and have fresh, summer corn in the winter. If you have a young, eager cook, this could be the recipe to include them in the kitchen.

6 tablespoons butter, melted
2 1/2 cups fresh corn (about 5 ears*)
2 large eggs
8 ounces sour cream

1/2 cup cornmeal
1 cup shredded Monterey Jack cheese
1 (4-ounce) can chopped green chilies
1 1/2 teaspoons salt

Preheat oven to 350 degrees. Grease a 9 x 9-inch baking pan.

In a large bowl mix the melted butter, corn, eggs, sour cream, cornmeal, cheese, chilies, and salt. Pour into the pan.

Bake for 50 to 55 minutes.

Makes 8 servings.

NOTE: For a lighter version, use low-fat sour cream.

* See page xx for my family's method of cutting off the cob.

FRIED CORN

This is the way my grandmother cooked sweet summer corn. Once you get the hang of cutting the corn (see page 99), this is a quick, easy, and delicious way to enjoy it fresh. You may need to cook it a couple of times before getting the consistency just the way your family likes it. I'll bet it will become a family favorite.

4 slices (about 3 1/2 ounces) bacon
4 cups fresh, sweet white or yellow corn
  (7 to 8 ears)

3/4 to 1 teaspoon salt
1/2 teaspoon black pepper
Water or milk as needed

In a cast-iron skillet or any heavy-bottomed skillet over medium heat, add the four pieces of bacon and cook until crisp. Be careful not to burn the bacon drippings.

Remove the cooked bacon from the skillet and drain on paper towels and immediately add the corn to the hot skillet. Add the salt and pepper and stir. Keep cooking the corn for about 10 minutes, stirring as the water begins to cook out. Taste the corn for salt and pepper seasoning and for doneness. Corn is done when you can no longer taste the starch, the kernels are tender, and the mixture is thickening but pourable. If the mixture gets too thick before it's done, add a little water or milk. The corn will cook properly if cut properly from the cob.

Makes 8 servings.

CUTTING THE CORN FROM THE COB

My mother and grandmothers would go to the farmers' market during the summer and buy bushels of corn. We would all be called on to help shuck. The corn was then cut from the cob, partially cooked, cooled, and frozen. It was delicious to have fried corn during the winter months. It was so good we were inspired to go back to the market the next summer and shuck all that corn again.

Shuck the corn, removing the husks and silks. Rinse the ears under cold running water. With a sharp knife and holding the ear over a bowl, cut just the tips of the kernels, letting them fall into the bowl. Turn the ear and continue taking the tips off until you've moved all around the ear. The next cut will be to take off about $2/3$ the height of the kernel, continuing around the ear. The next step is to scrape the remaining portion of the kernel into the bowl. The bottom part of the kernel is not cut off, but the "meat" left in the kernel is scraped off with the sharp edge of the knife. Now, just very briefly and lightly rinse the ear off with the water going into the bowl—not a lot of water but just to get a bit of the starch off the ear. This will give you a mixture of a majority of corn with a cup or so of water, which will "cook out" as the corn "fries."

FRIED OKRA

Long, green, funny looking pods . . . who would've thought they would fry up into golden, delicious little nuggets? A Southern delicacy, some cooks consider fried okra a big chore, but those who make it for their family are amply rewarded with big smiles and oohs and aahs. At Gabriel's, one of the first vegetables that customers' children learn to love is fried okra. There are many combinations of cornmeal, flour, seasonings, and frying methods. At Gabriel's, we deep-fry okra, but like many home cooks, my friend Lynda Ausburn uses what I call skillet frying. She doesn't use so much oil that it totally covers the okra in the pan.

1 cup buttermilk
2 cups self-rising flour
1 teaspoon salt
1/4 teaspoon cayenne pepper

1/4 teaspoon black pepper
1 pound okra, ends cut off
Vegetable oil or shortening for frying

Pour the buttermilk into a medium bowl. Combine the flour, salt, cayenne, and black pepper on a plate and mix well.

Slice the okra horizontally into 1/2-inch pieces.

Dip the slices into the buttermilk and then roll in the flour mixture.

In a skillet with deep sides, melt enough shortening to measure 1/2 to 3/4 inches deep. Heat until a pinch of flour sizzles in the oil when dropped in. Add the okra slices individually and cook until golden on the bottom side, 2 to 3 minutes. With a slotted spoon, turn the pieces over and brown on the other side, 2 to 3 minutes. When golden on both sides, remove with a slotted spoon and drain on paper towels.

If the bottom of the skillet begins to be covered with the browned flour from the okra, empty your skillet and begin again with clean oil. Serve warm.

Makes 4 servings.

NOTE: The fried okra can be held in a warm oven for a short while. My friend Nancy, who is a great cook, fries the okra to a light golden color, drains it on paper towels until cool, and then freezes it. She reheats it in the oven anytime she wants to whip up a vegetable dinner.

Fried Okra (page 101)

ROASTED BROCCOLI

Another good recipe from my friend Stephanie Ausburn. Her children are young, and she's teaching them early to enjoy the real flavor of the vegetable. The tiny bit of sugar aids in the caramelization of the broccoli.

....

1 bunch broccoli, washed and cut,   Kosher salt
   leaving 1 to 2 inches of stalk   Freshly ground pepper
Olive oil   1/2 teaspoon sugar

....

Move the oven rack to the lowest position. Preheat the oven to 500 degrees. Place a 9 x 13-inch jelly-roll pan on the lowest rack while the oven is preheating.

Cut the broccoli into large pieces. Place in a large bowl and drizzle with olive oil. Sprinkle generously with salt, pepper, and sugar. (The sugar helps the broccoli caramelize a little since broccoli has no natural sugar.) Toss the broccoli to evenly coat.

Pull the hot pan out of the oven and pour the broccoli on it immediately. It should sizzle as it comes in contact with the pan. Quickly spread the broccoli out so it's in an even layer and put the pan back in the oven on the lowest rack. Roast for 8 to 12 minutes, depending on how soft or crunchy you prefer the broccoli to be. The broccoli should start to turn brown on the tips. Remove from the oven and serve immediately.

Makes 6 to 8 servings.

PLAYING IN THE KITCHEN: I sometimes sprinkle lemon and/or freshly grated
  Parmigiano-Reggiano cheese on top.

HEAVENLY POTATOES

The name alone of this recipe from my friend Emily Teddy tempted me, and after reading the ingredients, I could hardly wait to taste them.

....

Potatoes
3 pounds Russet potatoes
Salt and black pepper to taste
1/4 cup (1/2 stick) butter, softened
1/2 cup milk

Topping
1/2 cup whipping cream
3 ounces Gruyere cheese, shredded
3 tablespoons freshly grated Parmesan
   cheese
Fresh parsley, chopped for garnish

....

Preheat the oven to 400 degrees.

Scrub the potatoes and prick with a fork. Place them directly on the oven rack and bake for 45 to 60 minutes, or until easily pierced with a fork. Remove from the oven, cool slightly, and halve lengthwise.

Spray a 9 x 13-inch or 3-quart casserole dish with nonstick cooking spray.

Scrape the potato flesh into a mixing bowl. Discard the peels or save to make fried potato skins. With a stand mixer or a potato masher, mash the potatoes until smooth. Taste the potatoes and add salt and pepper as needed. Add the butter and milk and stir until blended. Spread in the prepared dish.

Increase the oven temperature to 500 degrees.

To make the topping: In a medium bowl use a stand mixer to whip the cream to soft peaks. Fold in the Gruyere cheese with a plastic spatula. Spread the mixture evenly over the potatoes and sprinkle with Parmesan.

Bake until heated thoroughly and the topping is golden brown, about 10 minutes.

Garnish with parsley and serve warm.

Makes 8 to 10 servings.

Heavenly Potatoes (page 105)

WARM SWEET POTATO SALAD

Folks, we got lucky again. Chef Tom McEachern, the executive chef at our beautiful new Capital Grille in North Atlanta, is sharing several of his personal recipes with us. The sweet potato is loved in any number of ways by most Southerners. Here's one of Tom's suggestions.

1 gallon water
3 tablespoons salt
1 1/2 pounds Idaho potatoes, peeled and
    cut into 1-inch dice
1 1/2 pounds sweet potatoes, peeled and
    cut into 1-inch dice
1/3 cup balsamic vinegar

1/3 cup whole grain mustard
1/2 teaspoon salt
1/4 teaspoon black pepper
1 cup extra-virgin olive oil
4 large shallots, sliced
4 tablespoons fresh parsley, chopped
3 tablespoons capers

Pour the water into a large pot and add 3 tablespoons salt. Bring to a boil over high heat. Place the Idaho potatoes in the water, bring just to a simmer, and cook for 2 minutes. Add the sweet potatoes and continue to simmer for 7 additional minutes.

While the potatoes are cooking, make the vinaigrette. Whisk together the vinegar, mustard, salt, and pepper in a small bowl until the salt is dissolved. Gradually whisk in the olive oil, continuing to whisk until fully emulsified.

When the potatoes are done, drain them, rinse with cold water for 1 minute, and let them cool slightly. While the potatoes are still warm, add the sliced shallots, parsley, capers, and enough of the vinaigrette to coat the potatoes liberally.

Makes 10 to 12 servings.

PINK-EYED PEAS

My friend Lynda Ausburn likes pink-eyed peas and offered up this recipe. This seasoning should work on your favorite type of pea.

1 tablespoon butter
1/2 cup chopped onion
2 cloves garlic, minced
3 cups vegetable broth

3 cups pink-eyed peas, washed and cleaned
1/2 teaspoon black pepper
1/4 teaspoon smoked paprika
1 teaspoon salt

Melt the butter in a large skillet over medium heat. Add the onions and garlic and cook until the onions are clear. Add the broth, peas, pepper, paprika, and salt and cook for about 30 minutes or until the peas are tender.

Makes 6 to 8 servings.

SQUASH CASSEROLE

A Southern cookbook just has to have a squash casserole recipe. Squash is one of the most requested casseroles that we make for lunch at Gabriel's. I cooked and ate it every way but pickled to find the best dish. This is my favorite.

2 to 2 1/2 pounds yellow squash, washed and sliced
1 medium onion, medium to large dice
3 tablespoons dried parsley
1/4 cup milk

1 teaspoon salt
1/2 teaspoon black pepper
2 cups saltine or round butter cracker crumbs, divided
1 cup shredded Cheddar cheese

Preheat the oven to 450 degrees.

Put the squash and onions on a cookie sheet and place in the oven. Roast until tender, 10 to 15 minutes.

Turn the oven down to 350 degrees.

Coat a 9 x 13-inch casserole dish with nonstick cooking spray.

In a medium bowl mix the squash and onion, parsley, milk, salt and pepper, and 1 cup of cracker crumbs.

Place the mixture in the prepared dish. Combine the remaining cracker crumbs and the cheese and spread over the top of the casserole.

Bake for 25 minutes.

Makes 8 servings.

PLAYING IN THE KITCHEN: Here's an alternate cooking method. Place the squash and onions in a 2-quart saucepan and just barely cover with water. Bring to a boil over medium heat and simmer until tender, 15 to 20 minutes. Drain well.

COKE AND CHERRY CONGEALED SALAD

What could be more Southern than a congealed salad made with Coke? Maybe a Coke and a smile? This is a family favorite of my friend Glynda Chalfant.

1 (6-ounce) package cherry gelatin
1 (14.5-ounce) can tart cherries
1/2 cup water
1 cup sugar

1 (20-ounce) can crushed pineapple
  with juice
1 cup pecans, sliced or whole
1 (6-ounce) cola, room temperature

Put the dry gelatin mix in a large bowl. Drain the cherry juice into a medium saucepan, reserving and setting aside the cherries. Add the water and sugar to the saucepan and bring to a boil over high heat.

Pour the sugar water mixture over the gelatin and stir. Add the cherries, the can of pineapple and the juices, the pecans, and the cola. Stir well to combine and pour into a 9 x 13-inch casserole dish. Refrigerate for 3 to 4 hours to jell before serving.

Store in the refrigerator.

Makes 10 to 12 servings.

Orange Congealed Salad

Congealed salads are real favorites for potlucks and family gatherings. Always refreshing in the summer and colorful during holidays, the gelatin salad is a tasty way to get fruit on the table. This recipe is from the collection of my friend Caroline Teague and is still enjoyed and prepared by good cooks in the Teague/Ausburn family.

1 (8-ounce) can crushed pineapple, undrained
1 (6-ounce) package orange gelatin
1 cup cottage cheese
1/2 cup milk

1/4 cup mayonnaise
1/4 cup walnuts or pecans, optional
Leaf lettuce to line the serving plate, optional

In a medium saucepan over medium heat, combine the pineapple and gelatin. Stir to dissolve the gelatin.

Set aside long enough to cool.

Add the cottage cheese, milk, mayonnaise, and nuts.

Pour into a 2-quart casserole dish or mold and refrigerate until firm, about 4 hours.

To unmold, fill the sink with 2 to 3 inches of hot water. Dip the bottom of the mold into the water for 30 seconds. Using a sharp pointed knife, loosen the edge of the gelatin from the side of the mold. Invert the mold onto a serving plate. Serve cold. Refrigerate leftovers for up to 2 days.

Makes 8 servings.

LIME CONGEALED SALAD

Caroline Teague's family remembers the congealed salads she made for their gatherings. Who would have thought to combine gelatin and cottage cheese? Our mothers and grandmothers did!

2 cups water
1 (6-ounce) package lime gelatin
1 (8-ounce) carton cottage cheese
1/2 cup pecans, chopped

1 (20-ounce) can crushed pineapple, undrained
Leaf lettuce to line the serving plate, optional

Bring 2 cups of water to a boil in a small saucepan over high heat. Sprinkle the gelatin into a large bowl. Add the hot water and stir until the gelatin dissolves.

While the gelatin is cooling, combine the cottage cheese, nuts, and pineapple in a medium bowl and mix thoroughly. When the gelatin has cooled to the point that the bowl is just warm to the touch, add the cheese mixture and stir well to combine.

Pour into a 2-quart casserole dish or mold. Refrigerate until firm, about 4 hours.

To unmold, fill the sink with 2 to 3 inches of hot water. Dip the bottom of the mold into the water for 30 seconds. Using a sharp pointed knife, loosen the edge of the gelatin from the side of the mold. Invert the mold onto a serving plate and serve cold. Refrigerate leftovers for up to 3 days.

Makes 8 servings.

FIELD PEAS WITH SNAPS

My grandmother used to say she was cooking up a "mess" of peas. She'd serve them at Sunday lunch with cornbread and often fried chicken or ham and several other vegetables. Fresh peas and snaps come in during the later summer months, and there are a lot of varieties from which to choose. These days we can buy good fresh, frozen peas all year long and don't have to wait for summer. If you shell them yourself and have some smaller, less mature pods, break off the ends of the pods and snap the pod into 1 1/2-inch lengths to cook along with the peas. This adds a different texture and another color to your dish, along with a little more fiber.

4 cups fresh shelled peas
2 1/2 cups chicken stock or water

2 ounces salt pork* or bacon pieces cut
 into fourths
Salt and black pepper to taste

Wash the peas and carefully pick them over to discard any damaged peas. Put the peas in a pot and cover with water or stock. Add the salt pork or bacon pieces. Bring to a boil over medium-high heat. A lot of foam will accumulate on the top of the water; just skim it off. When the foaming stops, reduce the heat to low and simmer for 30 minutes, but don't let the peas get mushy.

Taste for seasoning. The amount of salt you will need to add will depend on how salty your seasoning meat or cooking stock is. Season with salt and pepper.

Serve hot with cornbread, fresh sliced tomatoes, and a few slices of sweet onion.

Makes 6 to 8 servings.

---

* When my mom used salt pork to cook her vegetables she would make several slashes with a knife in the fat part of the meat, cutting right up to the rind. The meat stayed in one piece but exposed more of the fatty part to render more flavor.

Field Peas with Snaps (page 115)

SAVING BACON GREASE

No kitchen should be without a container to save bacon grease. I remember my mom had a special metal canister that was specifically for bacon drippings (I think now they are referred to as renderings). It was equipped with its own strainer in the top to catch the little pieces of bacon, but I think that just took away some of the flavor.

My dad made his own breakfast every morning. He cooked a couple slices of bacon in a black iron skillet, then fried two eggs in the bacon drippings. Any leftover grease was poured into the canister that sat beside the stove.

Southerners have been recycling bacon drippings for years. Once cooled and solidified, we use it to grease the muffin tins or the skillet for cornbread or supplement the oil we use for frying some foods. Adding some portion of bacon grease to the skillet when making fried green tomatoes enhances the already good flavor of the dish. When making cornbread, I heat bacon drippings in my cast-iron skillet and pour them sizzling into the mix, then immediately pour the batter into the skillet to get a great brown crust.

My Grandmother Howell made the most delicious wilted mustard salad. She fried her bacon and drizzled the very hot drippings over the mustard greens. Chopped bacon, boiled eggs, and red onion on mustard greens was a real treat. It's more commonly done now using spinach leaves.

A heat-proof glass jar (such as a canning jar) is the best way to store bacon drippings. Cool them in the pan and while still liquid, pour them into the container. If they are kept for a long period of time they will go rancid, so storing in the refrigerator for infrequent usage is best. Freezing is an option also . . . just don't let them go to waste.

**A southern staple
on any table**

Fried Green Tomatoes

These are certainly a Southern classic. A slice of fried green tomato with a dipping sauce is often seen on menus in the South. I've eaten them with buttermilk ranch, a remoulade, or horseradish. All easily found at the grocery.

1/2 cup all-purpose flour
1/2 cup cornmeal
1 teaspoon salt
1/2 teaspoon black pepper
1/4 teaspoon cayenne pepper

2 to 3 green tomatoes, sliced 1/4-inch thick
4 tablespoons bacon grease
4 tablespoons vegetable oil and more as needed to replenish as you fry

Preheat the oven to 200 degrees. Line an ovenproof plate with paper towels.

In a shallow pan combine the flour, cornmeal, salt, black pepper, and cayenne pepper, stirring well to combine.

Dip each slice of green tomato into the flour mixture, coating both sides, and set on a plate.

In a large skillet add the bacon grease and vegetable oil and heat over medium heat until a pinch of the flour mixture sizzles when dropped into the oil.

Carefully slide each tomato slice into the hot oil and fry until golden brown, 3 to 4 minutes. Turn once and fry on the other side 2 minutes or until golden. Drain on a paper towel—lined ovenproof plate. Fry in batches if necessary. Place the finished slices on the paper towel—lined plate and keep warm in the oven.

Fried Green Tomatoes (page 119)

THREE-BEAN BAKE

Here's a tasty and filling side, perfect for a covered dish cookout or one of those cold weather tailgate parties. Dixie Bowden, one of my daughter Laura's teachers at the Walker School in Marietta, shared this recipe with me.

1/2 pound ground round
1 small onion, chopped
6 slices uncooked bacon, chopped
1 (15-ounce) can pork and beans, undrained
1 (15.5-ounce) can lima beans, rinsed and drained

1 (15-ounce) can kidney beans, rinsed and drained
1/2 cup firmly packed brown sugar
1/2 cup ketchup
1/2 cup barbecue sauce
1 teaspoon dry mustard

Preheat the oven to 375 degrees. Lightly grease a 1 1/2-quart casserole dish.

In a large skillet over medium-high heat, cook the ground round, onion, and bacon, stirring until the meat is no longer pink. Pour into a colander to drain the fat off. Return to the skillet and stir in the pork and beans, lima beans, kidney beans, brown sugar, ketchup, barbecue sauce, and dry mustard.

Pour the mixture into the dish. Bake for 45 to 55 minutes.

Makes 8 to 12 servings.

NOTE: For a gravy to serve over the chicken and dressing, see page 155.

PLAYING IN THE KITCHEN: Serve as a side or add a salad, fruit, or vegetables and you've got a full meal.

CORNBREAD DRESSING

Susan Danforth, a really good Southern cook, says this is the easiest cornbread dressing she has ever made. And it's really good!

Cornbread
2 cups self-rising cornmeal
1 cup self-rising flour
1 medium onion, chopped
3 large eggs
2 cups buttermilk

Dressing
1 quart water
1/2 cup (1 stick) butter
1 teaspoon salt
1/2 teaspoon black pepper
2 teaspoons celery seeds
2 whole chicken breasts, cut into 4
    pieces
2 teaspoons sage

To make the cornbread: Preheat the oven to 425 degrees. Grease a 2-quart baking pan.

In a large bowl mix the cornmeal, flour, onion, eggs, and buttermilk until it forms a slightly lumpy batter. Pour into the baking pan and bake for 30 minutes until brown. This can be made the day before you make the dressing.

To make the dressing: In a stockpot combine 1 quart of water, butter, salt, pepper, and celery seeds. Bring to a light boil over medium heat. Add the chicken breasts, turn the heat down to low, and cook the chicken breasts for 15 to 20 minutes, or until the chicken is tender. Remove the chicken breasts from the pot and set aside the liquid for broth.

Let the chicken cool until you can handle it, pull meat off the bones, and chop. Discard the bones.

Strain the broth through a fine-mesh strainer with a piece of cheesecloth or a coffee filter.

Preheat the oven to 350 degrees. Grease a 2-quart casserole dish.

In a large bowl crumble the cornbread, into bite-size pieces, add the chicken, broth, and sage and mix well. Pour into the dish and bake for 40 minutes until set and slightly browned.

Makes 8 to 12 servings.

Cornbread Dressing (page 123)

Pinto Beans

Every culture has their own dried bean associated with its culinary heritage, and the pinto is just one of the beans Southerners love. Once thought to be associated with low-budget eating, it is now hailed for its health benefits and good protein supply. When the recession began in late 2007, we added a "beans and greens" meal to the menu at Gabriel's. It included a bowl of pintos, a bowl of collards, a piece of cornbread, and iced tea. It's still a popular item in 2013.

5 to 6 slices uncooked bacon, dice medium
1 small onion, dice small
1 small green bell pepper, dice small

1 pound dried pinto beans, washed and picked through
1 1/8 teaspoon salt
1/4 teaspoon black pepper

In a stockpot over medium heat, add the bacon, onions, and bell pepper and sauté until the onions are clear and the bacon is cooked. Turn the heat to low, add the dried beans, and cover the beans with water plus 2 to 3 additional cups. Add the salt and pepper and stir to combine. Bring to a boil and continue to simmer uncovered on low for 1 1/2 to 2 hours.

Check from time to time to be sure the water hasn't cooked out. Add a cup at a time to keep the beans covered, if needed.

Makes 6 to 8 servings.

PLAYING IN THE KITCHEN: Use some chicken stock in place of the water to add a bit more richness.

DEVILED EGGS

Here's a Southern classic that has so many variations. My mom kept it really simple with the following recipe, using items she usually kept in her refrigerator.

12 large eggs, hard-boiled and peeled
1/2 cup mayonnaise
3 tablespoons sweet pickle relish

1 1/2 teaspoons prepared mustard
Salt and white pepper to taste
Paprika for garnishing

Cut the eggs in half lengthwise and put the yolks in a medium bowl.

Place the egg white halves on an egg tray or serving plate.

Mash the yolks with a fork. Add the mayonnaise, pickle relish, and mustard. Stir to combine well. Add the salt and pepper.

Fill the egg halves with the yolk mixture. Sprinkle lightly with paprika.

Serve immediately or cover and store in the refrigerator for up to 3 days.

Makes 24 halves.

PLAYING IN THE KITCHEN:

▶ Bacon Balsamic Deviled Eggs

12 large hard-boiled eggs, peeled
4 slices of crisply cooked bacon,
    crumbled
1/2 cup mayonnaise
1/4 cup minced red onion

1 1/4 teaspoon sugar
2 teaspoons balsamic vinegar
1/4 teaspoon celery salt
1/4 teaspoon black pepper
1/4 cup chopped fresh parsley for garnish

Cut the eggs in half lengthwise. Place the yolks in a small bowl and the egg white halves on a serving plate. Mash the yolks with a fork. Add the bacon, mayonnaise, onion, sugar, balsamic vinegar, celery salt, and black pepper. Mix well. Fill the egg halves evenly with the yolk mixture and sprinkle with parsley. Serve immediately or store covered in the refrigerator up to 3 days.

Makes 24 halves.

▶ Bacon Cheddar Deviled Eggs

12 large eggs, hard-boiled and peeled
1/2 cup buttermilk ranch dressing
1 cup crisply cooked chopped bacon

1/8 teaspoon salt
1/8 teaspoon black pepper
1 cup shredded Cheddar cheese

Cut the eggs in half lengthwise and place the yolks in a small bowl and the egg white halves on a serving plate. Mash the yolks with a fork. Add the ranch dressing, bacon, salt, pepper, and cheese to the egg yolks. Mix well. Fill egg white halves with yolk mixture. Serve immediately or store covered in the refrigerator until ready to serve. Keeps refrigerated up to 3 days.

Makes 24 halves.

▶ Avocado Deviled Eggs

9 large hard-boiled eggs, peeled
1/4 teaspoon prepared mustard
3 tablespoons mayonnaise
1 tablespoon pickle relish
Pinch of salt

Pinch of black pepper
Pinch of garlic powder
1/4 teaspoon hot sauce
1 avocado, mashed and finely chopped
Roma tomato chopped for garnish

Cut the eggs in half lengthwise and place the yolks in a small bowl and the egg white halves on a serving plate. Mash the yolks with a fork. Add the mustard, mayonnaise, pickle relish, salt, pepper, garlic powder, and hot sauce to the yolks. Mix well. Add the avocado and mix. Fill the egg white halves with the mixture and garnish with chopped tomatoes.

Makes 18 halves.

TIP: For an elegant look, put the yolk mixture into a piping bag fitted with a star tip and generously fill the egg halves.

TAKE IT TO THE TOP SHELF: Leave out the pickle relish and prepare as original recipe and garnish with thinly sliced smoked salmon, red or black caviar, or capers.

COLE SLAW

There are as many versions of cole slaw as there are local mom and pop diners and barbecue joints in the South. Some people chop the cabbage and some thinly slice it. Some like theirs slightly sweet, while others prefer a little heat. And then there's the mayonnaise-versus-oil-and-vinegar debate. However you prefer your cole slaw, don't hesitate to add a crisp vegetable of your choice, maybe radishes or grated sweet apples. It's a great way to eat your veggies and is a tasty side dish.

2 1/2 tablespoons cider vinegar
1/3 cup vegetable oil*
1 1/2 tablespoons sugar
3/4 teaspoon salt
1/2 teaspoon black pepper
1/4 teaspoon celery seeds

6 cups chopped or shredded green
 cabbage
1/4 cup chopped red, yellow, or green
 bell pepper
1/2 cup shredded carrot
1/2 cup grated red apple, optional

In a large bowl whisk the vinegar, oil, sugar, salt, pepper, and celery seeds until well combined and the sugar is dissolved.

Add the cabbage, bell peppers, carrot, and apple. Toss well. Cover and place in the refrigerator for about 30 minutes before serving to allow the flavors to combine.

Makes 8 servings.

PLAYING IN THE KITCHEN: Add radishes, purple cabbage, sweet onion, or your favorite veggie.

* For a mayonnaise-based cole slaw, substitute 1/4 to 1/2 cup mayonnaise for the oil.

How to Boil an Egg

People often refer to inadequate cooks as those who "can't even" boil an egg, but boiling them properly is actually harder than you think. Your finished egg should yield a bright golden yellow yolk instead of one that has a green ring around the edge. Here's how to boil a perfect egg every time: Place the number of eggs you want to boil in the appropriate-size saucepan. Cover the eggs with water. Place the saucepan over medium heat and bring to a moderately rolling boil. Cover the pan and remove it from the heat. Allow the pan to sit for 12 to 14 minutes. Pour the hot water out of the pan and fill the pan with cold water. Let the eggs sit, covered with cold water, until they are cool enough to handle. Crack the shells and peel. Place in a covered bowl and refrigerate until ready to use.

MACARONI AND CHEESE

Macaroni and cheese is one of the most popular sides that we serve at Gabriel's. From time to time I think about fun things to do with this staple recipe. This time I added tomatoes, bacon, and Monterey Jack cheese.

1 (12-ounce) box elbow macaroni
1/2 cup (1 stick) butter
1 teaspoon dry mustard
1/2 cup all-purpose flour
1/2 cup chopped sweet onion
3 cups whole milk
10 ounces Monterey Jack cheese, shredded

10 ounces extra-sharp Cheddar cheese, shredded
1 teaspoon salt
1/2 teaspoon white pepper
5 Roma tomatoes, cored and chopped
1 cup chopped cooked bacon
35 to 40 saltine or round butter crackers
2 tablespoons butter, melted

Preheat the oven to 350 degrees. Coat a 9 x 13-inch casserole dish with nonstick cooking spray.

Cook macaroni according to package directions for about 5 minutes, stirring occasionally until the macaroni is al dente. Drain the macaroni and set aside.

Dry the pot and return it to the stovetop over medium heat. Add the butter and melt. Add the dry mustard, flour, and onions, stirring constantly, and cook to a golden-colored roux. Whisk in the milk and allow to simmer for 5 to 6 minutes or until thickened, stirring often. Remove the mixture from the heat. Combine the cheeses and set aside 1 1/2 cups. Add the remaining cheese mixture to the roux and stir until completely melted. Add the salt and pepper. Return the macaroni to the pot and stir to combine and coat all of the macaroni. Fold the tomatoes and bacon into the mixture.

Pour the macaroni mixture into the prepared dish. Sprinkle the reserved 1 1/2 cups of cheese on top.

Break the crackers into fine crumbs using a food processor or put them into a resealable plastic bag and crush with a rolling pin until they are fine pieces. Add the melted butter.

Sprinkle the cracker mixture over the top of the casserole. Bake for 35 to 40 minutes or until the mixture is bubbly and lightly browned.

Makes 10 to 12 servings.

Macaroni and Cheese (page 135)

Dinner Jacket Potato Salad

Gail Schwartz, a Bible study friend of mine, is known for her delicious dishes she brings to our potluck suppers. Southerners love a good potato salad.

3 pounds new red potatoes
1 cup green olives, sliced
4 to 5 tablespoons chopped chives

Garlic salt to taste
1 cup mayonnaise*

Fill a large saucepan with the unpeeled potatoes and cover with water. Bring to a boil over high heat, lower the temperature to a simmer, and cook for 15 to 20 minutes, or until easily pierced with a fork. Drain well and allow to cool. When cool enough to handle, cut the potatoes into cubes and place in a large bowl. Fold in the olives, chives, garlic salt, and mayonnaise, using just enough of the 1 cup to coat potatoes.

Serve warm or refrigerate until ready to serve cold. This can be prepared a day ahead of serving.

Makes 6 to 8 servings.

* Gail uses Hellman's mayonnaise, but feel free to use your family's favorite.

MAIN DISHES

❧

Gabriel's Shrimp and Grits

Seafood Gumbo

Bourbon Marinated Pork Tenderloin

JB's Chili

Pepper Steak with Rice

Pork Chops and Rice

Honey Graham Sea Scallops

Zesty Lemon Chicken

Fried Chicken and Brown Gravy

Crispy Crusty Fish

Smothered Steak, Gravy, and Onions

Country Fried Steak

Chicken Enchiladas

Penne Pasta and Brie

Applewood Bacon, Caramelized Tomatoes,
and Arugula over Pasta

Chicken Piccata

Crispy Carolina Flounder
with Grilled Lemon-Thyme Vinaigrette

Pot Roast

Eggplant Soufflé

Shrimp and Corn Salad

❧

GABRIEL'S SHRIMP AND GRITS

This is Chef Gregg Baker's recipe. He has a knack for creating great flavor while still keeping it simple. Thanks, Gregg!

4 to 5 tablespoons vegetable oil
1 1/4 pounds medium (26/30)* shrimp
1 cup diced red, green, and yellow bell
  peppers
1 cup diced yellow onions
1 cup cooking sherry
1 teaspoon minced garlic

1 cup heavy cream
1 teaspoon salt
1 teaspoon black pepper
4 cups cooked Gabriel's Grits (recipe on
  page 7)
4 fresh basil leaves, finely chopped

Heat the oil in a large skillet over medium heat. Add the shrimp and cook for 30 seconds on each side.

Add the bell peppers and onions and cook until translucent.

Add the sherry and garlic and continue to cook for 30 more seconds.

Add the heavy cream, stir, and reduce until it forms a creamy sauce.

Add the salt and pepper.

Serve over grits and top with fresh basil.

Makes 4 servings.

* This number is another way to state the size of the shrimp, i.e., it requires 26 to 30 shrimp of this size to weigh a pound.

Gabriel's Shrimp and Grits (page 143)

Roux

A roux is a combination of fat and flour slow cooked to varying stages of color and flavor. The purpose of the roux is to thicken the mixture to which it is added and to add a nutty flavor. The longer the fat and flour are cooked and stirred, the darker the mixture becomes. A dark roux is used in the Seafood Gumbo on page 146. A light blond or white roux is used in soups or sauces and for the sausage gravy recipe on page 13. Both require constant stirring during the cooking process.

Dark Roux

1/2 cup canola or olive oil, butter, or bacon drippings

1 cup all-purpose flour or 1 1/2 cups for a thicker roux

In a very heavy skillet or pot, on low heat, whisk the fat and flour, cooking and stirring constantly until the mixture changes from a light to dark brown, 30 to 45 minutes. Add the remaining ingredients of dish.

White or Blond Roux

Use the same ingredients and quantities and follow the same steps as for a dark roux, but cook only to a light brown.

SEAFOOD GUMBO

The Gulf Coast has such a rich and colorful food history. Not many occasions take place without delicious food being present. My friend Liz Cole grew up in Biloxi, Mississippi, and then later lived in Ocean an Springs. Both cities offer a rich regional culture of arts and food. This is Liz's favorite seafood gumbo. Serve it with a loaf of fresh French bread.

1/2 cup all-purpose flour
1/2 cup olive oil, divided
1/2 cup chopped celery
1 cup diced yellow onion
3/4 cup diced green bell pepper
1 tablespoon pureed garlic*
2 teaspoons hot sauce
1/4 tablespoon dried thyme
1/4 teaspoon dried oregano
1/4 teaspoon cayenne pepper
1/2 teaspoon salt

1/4 teaspoon white pepper**
1/4 teaspoon black pepper
3/4 cup chopped tomatoes
6 cups seafood stock***
1/2 pound okra, cut into 1/2-inch slices
1/2 pound Andouille sausage, coarsely chopped
1/2 pound shrimp, shelled and deveined
1 tablespoon gumbo file****
6 cups cooked white rice

Place the flour and 1/4 cup olive oil in a cast-iron Dutch oven over medium heat and make a dark brown roux (see page 145). Add the celery, onion, and bell pepper and cook until tender. Add the garlic, hot sauce, thyme, oregano, cayenne, salt, white pepper, and black pepper. Stir for 5 minutes. Add the tomatoes and stock and bring to a boil. Lower the heat and simmer for 15 minutes.

While the gumbo is simmering, heat the remaining 1/4 cup olive oil in a skillet over medium heat and sauté the okra for 10 minutes. Add it to the gumbo pot and cook for 5 more minutes. Add the sausage and shrimp.

In a small bowl mix the gumbo file with a tablespoon of warm water and make a paste. Stir into the gumbo. Continue simmering, uncovered, for 30 to 40 more minutes, stirring occasionally.

Spoon the rice into a bowl and ladle the gumbo over the rice. May be served in individual bowls.

Makes 6 to 8 servings.

NOTE FROM LIZ: "Sometimes I use the shrimp heads and shells to make a seafood broth. I also use clam juice (in the carton) to give more flavor if needed. I've been known to add a teaspoon or two of liquid crab boil as well for flavor. Get chummy with your local fishmonger and you might be able to snag a few fish heads to add an extra layer of depth to your stock."

* You can purchase pureed garlic at the grocery store or use a garlic press to create the same consistency.

** White pepper comes from the same peppercorn as black. The black peppercorn is picked while still green, then left to shrivel and turn black. The white is left to ripen on the plant and is picked before it turns red. The official word is that white pepper is a bit milder than black. If you don't have white pepper on hand, just substitute additional black pepper.

*** You can also use a seafood bouillon if you don't want to make your own stock.

**** Filé is a spicy herb made from the leaves of the sassafras tree. It is used in Creole cooking as a spice and a thickening agent.

Bourbon Marinated Pork Tenderloin

This interesting combination of ingredients results in a delightful pork tenderloin from my friend and recipe tester Emily Teddy. Reduce the marinade down for a great sauce.

2 1/2 pounds pork tenderloin, silver skin removed
2/3 cup soy sauce
1/2 cup bourbon
1/4 cup Worcestershire sauce
1/4 cup water

1/4 cup canola oil
4 cloves garlic, minced
3 tablespoons brown sugar
2 tablespoons freshly ground black pepper
1/2 teaspoon ground ginger
Salt and black pepper to taste

Rinse the tenderloins and pat dry. In a large bowl whisk the soy sauce, bourbon, Worcestershire, water, oil, garlic, brown sugar, black pepper, and ginger until thoroughly mixed. Place the meat in a large zip-top bag and cover with marinade. Seal and marinate in the refrigerator for 12 hours.

Preheat the oven to 350 degrees with the oven rack in the middle position.

Remove the pork from the bag, reserving the liquid to reduce for a sauce. Sprinkle the meat with salt and pepper. Place a heavy ovenproof skillet over high heat. When the skillet is hot enough that you cannot hold your hand over it for more than two seconds, sear the tenderloin on all sides. This helps to lock in the juices and increase the flavor. Remove the skillet from the heat and place in the oven to roast until instant-read thermometer registers 135 to 140 degrees, 20 to 25 minutes.

While the pork is roasting, pour the marinade in saucepan over low heat and reduce the liquid until it becomes thick enough to coat the back of a spoon, 10 to 15 minutes. If necessary, whisk a bit of cornstarch into 1/4 cup of cool water, pour into the marinade, and whisk to thicken. Be sure to cook long enough to rid it of any cornstarch flavor. Keep the mixture warm and pour over the pork when it comes out of the oven.

Remove the pork from the oven, tent with foil, and allow to rest for 10 to 15 minutes before cutting. Save the juices to pour back over tenderloin once it is cut.

Slice the pork and serve with the sauce poured over the meat or on the side.

Makes 6 to 8 servings.

JB's Chili

John Bednarowski is the sports editor for our local newspaper, the Marietta Daily Journal, *and also the husband of Mo Bednarowski, a pastry chef by training and an invaluable employee and friend at Gabriel's. Mo's recipe for chocolate whoopie pies and pumpkin whoopies were included in* Second Helpings. *Two good cooks in one family!*

3 tablespoons canola oil
2 medium yellow onions, diced
3 pounds ground chuck
2 (27-ounce) cans chili beans, undrained
2 (26.5-ounce) cans black beans, undrained
1 (15-ounce) can black beans, undrained
2 (15.5-ounce) cans Texas chili starter, undrained
3 (16-ounce) cans dark kidney beans, undrained

1 (24-ounce) jar medium salsa
1 (10-ounce) can diced tomatoes and chilies, undrained
1 box Carroll Shelby's Chili Kit (masa flour, spice packet, cayenne)
4 tablespoons Mexican chili powder
1 tablespoon ground cumin
1 tablespoon cayenne pepper
Shredded Cheddar cheese for serving
Tortilla chips for serving

Heat the canola oil in a large stockpot over medium heat and add the onions. Turn the temperature down to low, cover, and allow to sweat* for about 10 minutes. Add the ground chuck, break it up with the back of a spoon, and increase the temperature to medium heat, stirring every few minutes, for 10 to 15 minutes, or until the meat browns.

Add the undrained chili beans, black beans, chili starter, and kidney beans.

Add the salsa, tomatoes and chilies, chili kit, chili powder, cumin, and cayenne pepper. Stir well to combine.

Bring to a boil over medium heat, turn the heat to low, and simmer for 30 minutes.

Serve with shredded cheese and tortilla chips.

Makes 6 quarts.

* Sweating vegetables is simply cooking them over low heat in a small amount of fat in a covered pot. This causes them to soften and release their moisture but not to brown.

Pepper Steak with Rice

Lynda Ausburn says this recipe is one of her family favorites. I think it would fit the bill perfectly for any family in need of rib-sticking comfort food.

1 pound beef round steak
1 tablespoon paprika
2 tablespoons butter
2 cloves garlic, finely chopped
1 1/2 cups beef broth
1 cup chopped green onion

2 green bell peppers, cut into 1/2-inch
   strips
2 tablespoons cornstarch
1/4 cup water
1/4 cup soy sauce
2 large tomatoes, chopped
3 cups cooked rice

Pound the steak to 1/4-inch thickness.* Cut into strips and sprinkle with paprika. Allow to stand while you prepare the other ingredients.

In a large skillet over medium heat, melt the butter, being careful not to let it burn. Add the meat and brown. Add the garlic and cook for about 1 minute, being careful not to burn the garlic. Add the broth, bring to a boil, and simmer for 30 minutes.

Stir in the onions and green peppers. Cover and cook for another 5 minutes.

In a small bowl whisk together the cornstarch, water, and soy sauce until smooth. Add to the meat and cook uncovered until thickened, about 2 minutes.

Add the tomatoes, gently stir, and heat uncovered until the tomatoes are hot. Serve over rice.

Makes 6 servings.

* For easy cleanup (and to keep pieces of meat from flying all over your kitchen), put down a piece of plastic wrap, place the meat in the middle, and then place another piece of wrap on top. Use a mallet to pound the meat to the desired thickness. Then remove the plastic wrap and discard.

PORK CHOPS AND RICE

Sally Rhoden's mom served this to her family in Monroe, Georgia.

Salt and black pepper to taste
4 1/2 inch-thick pork chops
2 to 3 tablespoons oil
1 (12-ounce) can stewed tomatoes,
   undrained

2 green, red, or yellow bell peppers,
   cored and cut into rings
2 onions, sliced
2 cups white or brown instant rice
Salt and black pepper to taste

Lightly salt and pepper both sides of pork chop.

Heat the oil in a large skillet over medium heat.

Add the pork chops to the skillet and cook for 3 to 5 minutes on each side, until brown.

Pour the tomatoes around the chops. Add the bell pepper rings and slices of onion on top of each chop, and sprinkle each pork chop with rice. You may need to add more water so that the pork can stew.

Cover and cook over low heat for 20 to 30 minutes, occasionally spooning liquid onto the pork chops.

Add additional salt and pepper to taste. Serve hot.

Makes 4 servings.

Honey Graham Sea Scallops

Ed Gabriel's recipe for Scallops and Champagne Risotto was featured in Second Helpings, *and it's one of my favorite seafood entrees. You'll want to try this winner too!*

16 sea scallops*
2 large eggs, beaten lightly
1/2 sleeve honey graham crackers, finely crushed

Peanut or vegetable oil
Chipotle sauce or tartar sauce for serving

Clean the scallops by rinsing in cold water. Remove the muscle** and pat dry with a paper towel. Pour the eggs in a shallow dish. Spread the cracker crumbs over a dinner plate. Dip the scallops individually in the beaten eggs, then dredge in the cracker crumbs, rolling to coat completely.

Heat oil in a fryer or a skillet deep enough to hold enough oil to cover the scallops on high heat until it reaches 350 degrees on an instant-read thermometer. Lower the scallops into the hot oil and cook for approximately 1 1/2 to 2 minutes or until golden brown. Serve immediately with chipotle or tartar sauce or both.

Makes 4 servings.

* An average pound of sea scallops contains 10 (1 1/2- to 2-inch) scallops.
** The muscle (or foot) is on the side of the scallop. If the scallops you purchase haven't been cleaned already, just use a small, sharp knife to pull it off.

ZESTY LEMON CHICKEN

Kay Finney, a resident of Atlanta, Georgia, and good friend of Sally Rhoden, shared this recipe with me. This chicken is tender and delicious. The brown sugar adds another dimension of flavor.

6 boneless skinless chicken breasts,*
   halved
2 cups bottled lemon juice
1 cup all-purpose flour
2 teaspoons paprika
1 teaspoon black pepper
1 1/2 teaspoons salt

1/2 cup vegetable oil
2 tablespoons grated lemon peel
1/3 cup packed light brown sugar
1/4 cup chicken broth
2 thinly sliced lemons
Minced fresh parsley for garnish

Combine the chicken and lemon juice in a zip-top bag and refrigerate overnight.

Preheat the oven to 350 degrees.

Remove the chicken from the zip-top bag and pat dry. Discard the bag. In another bag combine the flour, paprika, pepper, and salt. Add the chicken and shake until coated.

Pour the oil into a large skillet over medium heat. When the oil is hot, fry the chicken until well browned on both sides, about 10 minutes total. Arrange the chicken in a single layer in a 9 x 13-inch casserole dish, then sprinkle evenly with lemon peel and brown sugar. Pour the chicken broth around the chicken. Place a thin lemon slice on top of each piece and sprinkle with minced parsley. Bake for 30 minutes or until tender.

Makes 10 to 12 servings.

* If the chicken pieces are large, pound them a bit before cutting in half.

Fried Chicken and Brown Gravy

I don't know of any dish more associated with Southern culture than fried chicken. Like sweet potato casserole, every family has their favorite. All of us can be as successful as Celia in the book The Help *with a little help and practice. Experiment with adding spices such as garlic powder, paprika, cayenne pepper, and others to find your family favorite. This is mine. It's as close to my mom's chicken as I can get without that aluminum lid she always used that I stupidly sent to the trash pile.*

1 whole chicken, cut into pieces (or pieces of your choice already cut and packaged)
1/4 cup plus 2 teaspoons salt, divided
2 cups buttermilk
2 cups all-purpose flour

2 teaspoons black pepper
1 teaspoon paprika
1/2 teaspoon poultry seasoning
1 to 1 1/2 quarts vegetable or peanut oil for frying
Brown Gravy (recipe follows)

An hour or so before you're ready to fry, rinse the chicken under cold water and pat dry with paper towels. Put the chicken in a large bowl. Add 1/4 cup salt to the buttermilk and stir. Pour the buttermilk over the chicken and set in the refrigerator for 1 hour to soak.

In a large zip-top plastic bag, mix the flour, remaining 2 teaspoons salt, pepper, paprika, and poultry seasoning.

Pour the oil in a large cast-iron skillet that has high sides, about halfway up the side of the skillet, and heat over medium-high heat.

While the oil heats, begin battering your chicken. Use tongs to transfer one piece of chicken at a time to the flour bag. When you have a few pieces in the bag, toss to coat well. Transfer the floured chicken pieces to a plate. Try to keep one hand dry for using the tongs and one hand for pulling chicken from the flour. Discard the buttermilk once you've battered all the chicken.

Use an instant-read thermometer to check the temperature of the oil. When your instant-read thermometer reads 350 to 360 degrees, you're ready to fry. If you don't have a thermometer, you can test the oil with a pinch of flour. It will sizzle in the oil when the oil is getting hot enough. Don't allow the oil to smoke.

Using clean tongs, carefully slide the largest pieces of chicken into the hot oil, skin side down and one piece at a time, until the pan is about three-fourths full.

The oil will start to cool off as you fill up the skillet. Keep the heat up sufficiently so that the oil will continue to bubble up around the chicken.

About 10 minutes into the process, cover the skillet with a lid and let the chicken steam for about 5 minutes. When the chicken has turned golden brown on the bottom, remove the lid and turn the pieces. Place the lid on for about 5 more minutes and allow the chicken to steam again. Remove the lid and let the chicken brown again, about 10 minutes. Try not to turn the chicken more than once as this will sometimes cause the crust to stick to the bottom of the pan instead of the chicken.

Remove the pieces to a paper towel—lined rack to let the pieces drain. Check the temperature of the leg portion to see if it registers at least 165 degrees on an instant-read thermometer. It should take about 25 minutes per batch. My mom knew instinctively when the chicken was done. She used a cooking fork and could tell just by sticking the chicken.

Repeat with remaining chicken. You may need to add additional oil or strain flour and batter that was left in the oil. Make sure the oil temperature comes back up to 350 degrees before you begin cooking again.

The chicken will hold at room temperature for up to an hour while you're frying the remaining pieces. Serve with Brown Gravy on the side.

Brown Gravy

After frying the chicken, my mom would make this brown gravy that my daddy liked to serve over rice or fresh biscuits. You can also serve it with your mashed potatoes. Whatever you do, don't let those yummy bits in the pan go to waste.

3 to 4 tablespoons oil used to fry chicken	2 cups water
3 to 4 tablespoons all-purpose flour	Salt and black pepper to taste

Once you've finished frying your chicken, leave 3 to 4 tablespoons of oil in the pan and add the flour. Heat over medium heat. The flour will begin to brown in the skillet. Once the flour is an even brown, pour the water into the skillet and whisk until the mixture is smooth. Season with salt and pepper and continue to stir and cook until the gravy reaches the desired consistency.

CRISPY CRUSTY FISH

When done well, fish is a healthy and delicious choice. My friend, Kay Phinney of Atlanta, who shared this recipe, adds some colorful vegetables to this dish. It comes together quickly and tastes as good as it looks. She usually uses fresh or frozen tilapia filets.

1 cup cherry tomatoes, halved
1 cup thinly sliced leeks, rinsed and drained
1/2 cup chopped green bell pepper
1 tablespoon minced garlic
1/2 cup Panko crumbs

1/2 cup grated Parmesan cheese
1/2 cup crushed plain potato chips
1/2 teaspoon paprika
1/4 teaspoon cayenne pepper
2 tablespoons melted butter
4 red snapper, tilapia, or halibut fillets

Preheat the oven to 450 degrees.

In a medium bowl combine the tomatoes, leeks, bell pepper, and garlic. Spread in the bottom of a 9 x 13-inch casserole dish.

In the same bowl you used to combine the vegetables combine the Panko, Parmesan cheese, potato chips, paprika, and cayenne. Add the melted butter and toss.

Divide the crumb mixture evenly over each fillet, pressing into the fish.

Arrange the fish on top of the vegetables. Season with salt and pepper.

Bake for 20 minutes or until the fish flakes easily when tested with a fork.*

Makes 4 servings.

---

* If the fish was prepared earlier and refrigerated, let it sit out of the refrigerator for 30 minutes to allow it to come to room temperature before preparing.

SMOTHERED STEAK, GRAVY, AND ONIONS

My mom made this often when we were growing up. She would serve it with rice or mashed potatoes. She added a green vegetable, and her dinner was complete. I mistakenly called this dish country fried steak at Gabriel's one day. One of the chefs corrected me and insisted on making a "real" country fried steak. We got accolades about the new country fried dish, but we also heard plenty of yowls about the disappearance of the old one. So now we do both at Gabriel's. We do our best to please all of the people all of the time.

4 (6-ounce) pieces eye of round steak or cubed steak
2 cups all-purpose flour
2 teaspoons salt, divided
1 teaspoon black pepper, divided
1/2 cup vegetable oil, divided
2 tablespoons olive oil
1 large onion, peeled and sliced into rings
4 cups beef stock, divided

If using eye of round steak, lay pieces of steak on a chopping board and tenderize with a meat mallet, beating to a 1/4-inch thickness. If you are using cubed steak, you can skip this step.

In a shallow baking dish combine the flour, 1 1/2 teaspoons salt, and 3/4 teaspoon pepper.

Dredge the slices of meat through the flour, coating both sides. Reserve 1/2 cup of the flour mixture.

Heat 7 to 8 tablespoons of vegetable oil in a cast-iron skillet over medium-high heat. Drop a pinch of flour in the oil to test. If it sizzles you're ready to fry the steaks. Using tongs, begin to add the dredged pieces of meat to the skillet. Cook on one side for 3 to 5 minutes and then turn to cook for 3 to 5 minutes on the other side. When both sides are nicely brown and crusted, transfer to a plate.

Add 2 tablespoons olive oil to the skillet so that you have 4 to 5 tablespoons of oil in skillet. Add the onions and sauté until transparent, about 5 minutes. Transfer to the plate with the steak.

If necessary, add 2 or 3 more tablespoons of oil to the skillet to have 4 to 5 tablespoons of oil in bottom of skillet. When the oil is hot, add the reserved seasoned flour to the skillet. Whisk and cook to a golden brown. When the flour is golden brown, pour in 3 cups beef stock and stir and cook to form a gravy. Season with the remaining $1/2$ teaspoon salt and $1/4$ teaspoon pepper.

Return the meat, onions, and any juices on the plate to the skillet and spoon the gravy over the steak. Cover the skillet and turn the heat to very low so that the mixture just simmers for about 1 hour. Stir four or five times from the bottom of the skillet to keep from sticking. Add the remaining 1 cup beef stock as needed to keep meat simmering in the liquid.

Makes 2 to 4 servings.

COUNTRY FRIED STEAK

This is one of our most frequently ordered entrees at Gabriel's. Whip up a white gravy to ladle over this steak and mashed potatoes.

2 1/3 cups all-purpose flour, divided
1 1/2 teaspoons salt
1 1/2 teaspoons black pepper
1 to 1 1/2 cups buttermilk

1 1/2 pounds eye of round roast, sliced
    into 6 (4-ounce) pieces, tenderized*
Vegetable oil for frying
Salt and black pepper to taste
2 cups whole milk, divided

Set up a work station to prepare the meat for frying. In a medium bowl combine 2 cups flour, salt, and pepper and mix well to distribute. Pour the buttermilk into the second bowl.

Dredge each piece of meat in the flour, covering both sides, then dip it in the buttermilk, wetting both sides. Dredge it again in the flour mixture and set the pieces on a plate or sheet pan until you have floured and dredged all pieces.

Once all the meat is floured, heat about 1/4 inch of oil in a large skillet over medium heat. The oil is ready when a pinch of flour dropped into the oil sizzles.

Ease each piece of meat into the hot oil until your skillet is full. You will probably have to work in two batches. Cook the meat for 3 to 4 minutes on each side, turning when golden brown. Some of the flouring will come off, but it will just serve to make the gravy better. Add more oil if needed when cooking the second batch.

When you have browned the meat on both sides, remove to a warm, paper towel–lined plate to hold while you make the gravy.

Pour off all but 1/4 cup of the grease and bits on the bottom of the pan. Over medium-low heat add 1/3 cup of flour. Whisk the flour into the oil until the flour turns a golden brown. Add 1/4 teaspoon of salt and pepper. Add 1 1/2 cups milk and whisk until the mixture is smooth and begins to thicken. Lower the heat and cook for 5 to 6 minutes, stirring and adding more milk as needed. Add more salt and pepper to taste if desired.

Serve each piece of steak with a ladleful of gravy over it. Pour any remaining gravy into a bowl and serve at the table.

Makes 6 servings.

TIP: When making smothered steak, the meat simmers in gravy for a good while and has an opportunity to become tender. Country fried steak is browned on both sides, the gravy is made, and the dish is served, so you really need a piece of meat that's a little more tender than a cube steak to begin the cooking process.

---

* If you didn't have the butcher or grocer tenderize the meat for you, you'll need to pound each piece on both sides with a meat tenderizer. Pound it enough that the pieces are significantly thinner and larger than you began with. When at the market, look at a cut of cubed steak to get an idea of how thick the pieces should be.

CHICKEN ENCHILADAS

Emily Teddy, an avid cook and young mom here in Marietta from Austin, Texas, has been recipe testing with me. Here's one of her TexMex recipes. She is Marietta's gain and Texas's loss for more reasons than her cooking ability! Enjoy!

1/2 cup (1 stick) butter
1 cup chopped onion
1 (4-ounce) can chopped green chilies
1/2 cup chicken broth
1/4 to 1/2 teaspoon hot sauce, to taste
1 (8-ounce) package cream cheese, softened

4 chicken breasts, cooked, boned, and diced (about 3 cups)
Salt and black pepper to taste
6 to 10 flour tortillas
1 1/2 cups whipping cream
1 1/2 cups shredded Monterey Jack cheese
Homemade or purchased salsa, optional

Preheat the oven to 350 degrees. Grease a 9 x 13-inch casserole dish.

In a skillet melt the butter and sauté the onion until transparent. Add the chilies, broth, and hot sauce. Add the cream cheese and stir until melted. Add the chicken, and salt and pepper to taste.

Fill the tortillas with the chicken mixture and roll. Place seam down in the casserole dish.

If any of the chicken mixture remains after filling the tortillas, spread it over the top of the enchiladas and then pour whipping cream over them. Cover with the cheese and spread the salsa on top. Cover and bake for 45 minutes.

Makes 6 to 8 servings.

Penne Pasta and Brie

Emily Teddy's family puts this dish together early in the day. When everyone is tired and hungry, all they have to do is cook the pasta and toss. It's a perfect dish after a day at the beach, but we all have days when we can use a convenient and delicious dish. Once you try it, I bet this will be one of yours.

1 bunch basil, chopped
1 scant cup olive oil
3 cloves garlic, diced
1/2 cup balsamic vinegar
1/2 teaspoon salt
1/4 teaspoon black pepper

1 (8-ounce) wedge brie, diced into 1/2-
   inch pieces
4 large ripe tomatoes, cut into chunks
   (about 6 cups)*
8 ounces penne pasta

In a large bowl whisk together the basil, olive oil, garlic, vinegar, salt, and pepper.

Add the brie and tomatoes. Cover and let marinate all day until ready to mix the cooked pasta in just before serving.

Thirty minutes or so before serving, cook the pasta according to package directions. Drain well, let cool just slightly, and add to the marinated brie and tomatoes, tossing to combine.

Makes 10 to 12 servings.

TIP: Add an easy tossed salad with a light vinaigrette for a complete meal.

* I love grape tomatoes and think they're tasty all year long. Instead of full-size tomatoes, add an equivalent of grape tomatoes cut in half.

Applewood Bacon, Caramelized Tomatoes, and Arugula over Pasta

This dish combines 3 of my favorite flavors. Frankly, caramelizing anything but sugar is a new experience for this Southern girl, but roasted, caramelized tomatoes are delicious. They just get sweeter! Arugula is a new flavor for me also. It has just the right amount of spice. Try this dish and I bet you'll feel the same way.

3 (14.5-ounce) cans diced tomatoes, undrained
7 tablespoons olive oil, divided
Salt and black pepper to taste
1 cup crushed tomatoes
1 large Vidalia or sweet onion
2 ears fresh yellow corn
1 pound box penne pasta

8 slices thick-sliced applewood smoked bacon, cut into 1/2-inch pieces
3 garlic cloves, minced
1/2 teaspoon dried crushed red pepper
1 1/2 cups reduced-sodium chicken broth
1 (5-ounce) bag arugula
1/2 cup Parmesan cheese, grated

Preheat the oven to 300 degrees.

Place the diced tomatoes in a large strainer set over a large bowl. Let stand for 15 minutes. With a large wooden spoon press the remaining liquid from the tomatoes into the bowl and reserve the juice for the sauce. Spray a 15 x 10-inch jelly-roll pan with a light coat of nonstick spray. Spread the tomatoes in a single layer over the pan, drizzle with 2 tablespoons of the olive oil, and sprinkle with salt and pepper. Roast the tomatoes for 45 minutes until lightly caramelized, stirring them every 15 minutes.

While the tomatoes are caramelizing, bring the reserved tomato juice and crushed tomatoes to a boil in a heavy medium saucepan over medium heat. Reduce the heat to low and simmer until reduced to 1 1/2 cups, about 30 minutes.

Cut the corn from the cobs. Heat 2 tablespoons olive oil in a large pot over medium heat. Add the onion and corn and sauté until the onion is translucent, about 5 minutes. Stir in the crushed tomatoes and roasted tomatoes.*

Bring a large pot of water to a boil over high heat. Add giant pinch of salt to the water before adding the pasta. Cook according to package directions.

Cook the bacon in a large heavy skillet over medium heat until crisp. Drain on paper towels. Pour off the drippings from the skillet. Heat the remaining 3 tablespoons oil in the skillet over medium heat. Add the garlic and red pepper and stir about 1 minute. Add the tomato sauce and chicken broth and simmer for 10 minutes to develop the flavors. Stir in the bacon.

Drain the pasta and return to the pot.

Add the sauce, arugula, and Parmesan cheese to the pasta. Toss until the arugula melts. Divide among six bowls. Serve with additional Parmesan cheese.

Makes 6 servings.

* The sauce can be made up to three days ahead. Cool, cover, and store in the refrigerator.

CHICKEN PICCATA

Good cooking runs in my friend Ginny McNabbs's family. She shared this recipe from Daniel and Kiley Hodge, her son and daughter-in-law. Chicken Piccata is one of my favorite dishes, and once I tested this recipe it became another go-to meal for putting something wonderful on the table with little effort. It's simple and full of good flavors. Serve it with a side of hot pasta mixed with a little olive oil and freshly grated Parmesan cheese.

2 boneless skinless chicken breasts,
    butterflied and cut in half (4 pieces)
Sea salt
Freshly ground black pepper
All-purpose flour for dredging
6 tablespoons butter, divided

5 tablespoons extra-virgin olive oil,
    divided
1/3 cup fresh lemon juice
1/2 cup chicken stock
1/4 cup capers, rinsed
1/3 cup chopped fresh parsley for garnish
1/2 lemon, thinly sliced for garnish

Rinse the chicken under cold water and pat dry with paper towels. Place the breasts on a cutting board and tenderize with a meat mallet or the dull edge of a heavy knife. Season both sides of chicken with salt and pepper.

Pour the flour into a shallow baking dish and dredge the chicken in flour. Shake off the excess.

In a large sauté pan over medium-high heat, melt 2 tablespoons of butter with 3 tablespoons of olive oil.* When the butter and oil start to sizzle, add 2 pieces of chicken and cook for 3 minutes. When the chicken is brown, turn and cook on the other side for 3 minutes. Transfer to a warm platter while you cook the remaining chicken pieces. Add 2 tablespoons of butter and the remaining 2 tablespoons of olive oil to the pan and allow to sizzle before adding the chicken. Transfer to the warm platter.

Return the pan to the heat and deglaze the pan with lemon juice, stock, and capers. Bring to a boil, scraping up the browned bits on the bottom of the pan for extra flavor. Check for seasoning and add salt and pepper as needed. (I add a little less than $^1/_2$ teaspoon sea salt and $^1/_8$ teaspoon black pepper.)

Return the chicken to the pan and simmer for 5 minutes. Remove the chicken to the warm platter. Add the remaining 2 tablespoons butter to the sauce and whisk vigorously. Pour the sauce over the chicken and garnish with parsley and a few lemon slices.

Makes 4 to 6 servings.

---

* Combining the butter and the oil for sautéing allows you to use a higher heat on the butter without it burning and still gives you the butter flavor.

CRISPY CAROLINA FLOUNDER WITH GRILLED LEMON-THYME VINAIGRETTE

Tom McEachern, the executive chef at Atlanta's newest Capital Grille, shared this personal recipe with us. Several of his recipes are in my first two books also. If you have tried those, you'll know how exciting it is to have more of his recipes!

Grilled Lemon-Thyme Vinaigrette*

6 lemons, halved
1/4 cup plus 1 tablespoon olive oil
5 tablespoons honey
3 tablespoons sherry vinegar
2 tablespoons plus 1 teaspoon chopped
    fresh thyme

1/4 cup minced shallots
1/4 cup vegetable oil
Pinch of salt and black pepper to taste

Preheat a grill pan over medium-high heat.

Brush the lemon halves with the 1 tablespoon of olive oil. Place the lemons cut side down on the grill pan and grill them enough to get a nice, caramelized color on them (be sure not to burn them).

Squeeze the lemons over a mesh strainer into a medium bowl. Add the honey, vinegar, thyme, and shallots. In a small bowl combine the 1/4 cup olive oil with the vegetable oil. Slowly whisk the oil into the lemon mixture. Add a pinch of salt and pepper.

Makes approximately 2 cups.

* Make the vinaigrette ahead of time. This vinaigrette can be used on salads, other types of fish, and poultry. It will keep in the refrigerator for up to 2 weeks.

Fish

6 (6-ounce) flounder fillets
1 teaspoon salt
Freshly ground pepper

1 can Wondra flour* to dust each fillet
2/3 cup olive oil

Dry and season each fillet with salt and pepper. Dust both sides of each fillet with the Wondra flour, making sure that there is good coverage.

Heat a cast-iron skillet or large skillet over medium-high heat. Add a few tablespoons of the olive oil. Once the pan is hot enough and the oil starts to smoke, add the first two pieces of fish and brown approximately 3 minutes on each side. While the fish cooks, prepare a cookie sheet with a double layer of paper towels. Transfer the fish to the paper towel–lined cookie sheet (do not stack the fish).

Wipe out the skillet, add a few more tablespoons of the olive oil, and heat until it begins to smoke. Add the next two pieces of fish and cook. Transfer to the cookie sheet and repeat with the final two fillets. Serve warm with the Grilled Lemon-Thyme Vinaigrette drizzled over each piece.

Makes 6 servings.

* Wondra flour is a very fine blend that gives the fish a consistent, light, and crispy crust.

POT ROAST

Pot roast is a staple in the average American household. My mom made a pot roast nearly every Saturday night for Sunday lunch, making sure to give it plenty of time to braise. She used a chuck roast, an inexpensive cut, but the extra marbling gave it extra flavor and tenderness. This was one of her magic dishes that could stretch into two different meals. The second was hash: potatoes, onions, and shredded leftover beef, along with the juices from the roast, all simmered in her cast-iron skillet and served with hot homemade biscuits. Below is my version of her pot roast.

1 tablespoon olive oil
1 tablespoon vegetable shortening
1 (3- to 4-pound) boneless chuck or
   rump roast
1 teaspoon kosher salt
1/4 teaspoon freshly ground black pepper
All-purpose flour for dredging
2 cups chopped onions
1 cup dry red wine
1 cup beef broth

1 cup water
4 thyme sprigs
3 garlic cloves, chopped
1 bay leaf
8 medium carrots, peeled and cut
   diagonally into 2-inch pieces
3 pounds Yukon gold potatoes, peeled
   and cut into 4 wedges each
Salt and black pepper to taste

Preheat the oven to 300 degrees.

Heat the olive oil and shortening in a large Dutch oven over medium-high heat.

Sprinkle the chuck roast with salt and pepper and dredge in the flour, coating all sides of the roast.

Add the roast to the hot pan and cook, turning to brown on all sides. Be sure not to burn the fat. Use tongs to turn without piercing the meat if possible.

Remove the roast from the pan. Turn the heat down to medium and add the onions to pan and sauté until tender. Scrape the bottom of the pan to loosen any particles sticking to pan.

Return the roast to the pan and add the red wine. In a small bowl mix the beef broth and water. Add to the pan to cover about two-thirds up the sides of meat. Add the thyme, chopped garlic, and bay leaf. Bring to a simmer, cover, and carefully move the pan to the oven. Bake for 1 1/2 to 2 hours or until the roast is almost tender. Occasionally check to be sure all the liquid has not cooked out. Add more broth or water if needed.

Add the carrots and potatoes to the pan. Cover and cook an additional 45 minutes to an hour or until the vegetables are fork-tender. Remove the thyme sprigs and bay leaf from the pan and discard. Remove the meat and vegetables from the pan. If lots of liquid is left, set the pan over medium heat and simmer until the liquid is reduced to a nice serving consistency. Taste for seasoning and salt and pepper as needed. While the gravy is simmering, use two forks to break the meat into serving-size pieces. Place the meat and vegetables onto a serving plate and drizzle with some of the liquid from the pan. Pour any remaining gravy into a serving bowl or gravy boat for passing at the table.

Makes 6 to 8 servings.

Eggplant Soufflé

I am a big fan of eggplant. This is now one of my favorite ways to enjoy it. I love having the leftovers for lunch.

3 small to medium eggplants, peeled and cut into cubes
6 tablespoons butter, divided
2 medium white onions, sliced thinly
3/4 teaspoon salt

1/2 teaspoon black pepper
8 ounces shredded Cheddar cheese
2 large eggs, beaten
3 Roma tomatoes, peeled and diced
1 1/2 cups Italian bread crumbs

Preheat the oven to 250 degrees. Spray a 2-quart casserole dish lightly with nonstick spray.

Fill a 2- or 3-quart saucepan with enough water to cover the eggplant. Bring to a boil over medium-high heat and cook until tender, about 10 minutes. Drain very well.

While the eggplant is cooking, add 2 tablespoons butter to a large skillet over medium-high heat. Add the onions and cook until they are translucent. Remove from the heat.

In a large bowl combine the hot, well-drained eggplant, onions, salt, pepper, cheese, and eggs.

Spoon the eggplant mixture into the dish. Sprinkle the tomatoes over the eggplant mixture, spread the bread crumbs over the tomatoes, and dot with the remaining 4 tablespoons of butter. The consistency should not be soupy.

Bake for 2 hours. Serve warm.

Makes 8 servings.

Shrimp and Corn Salad

Southerners love shrimp and they love corn. Together they're awesome! Perfect for brunch, lunch, or as an appetizer, this recipe is courtesy of Gregg Baker.

1 teaspoon kosher salt, divided
1 1/2 lemons, halved and divided
2 pounds (18/26 count) frozen shrimp, peeled with tail
2/3 cup diced red onion
2/3 cup diced celery

2 tablespoons plus 1 teaspoon chopped fresh dill
2 cups plus 2 tablespoons frozen yellow corn kernels, uncooked
1 1/3 cups mayonnaise
French bread or baguette, sliced 1/4 inch thick

In a large pot bring a half gallon of water to a boil over medium-high heat. Add 1/2 teaspoon of salt and the juice and rinds of 1 lemon. Let boil a couple of minutes.

Reduce the heat to medium-low and add the shrimp. Simmer for 3 to 5 minutes or until the shrimp are bright pink and the tails curl. Using a slotted spoon, remove the shrimp from the poaching liquid and let cool enough to handle.

Remove the tails and chop the shrimp into 3 pieces.

Fill a bowl with very hot tap water and drop the corn kernels in. Let sit for 4 or 5 minutes. Drain well.

In a large bowl combine the juice from the remaining 1/2 lemon, red onion, celery, dill, corn, the remaining 1/2 teaspoon kosher salt, and mayonnaise and whisk. Add the shrimp to the mixture and stir to coat the shrimp and corn well. Cover and chill in refrigerator until ready to serve.

Toast the bread slices on both sides and let cool. The bread can be toasted ahead of time and stored in an airtight container until ready to serve. Serve with shrimp.

Makes 8 to 10 servings.

SWEETS

CAKE POPS

Cake on a stick. Who would have thought? I like cake almost any way it's presented to me. It's not just kids who love them. All cake lovers do!

Initially at Gabriel's, we used any extra layers that we might have from a day of baking for cake pops. They are so loved now we bake layers just for cake pops.

They are really a fun cooking project to do with children, and there are so many ways to make them festive. Tinting the color of white chocolate for dipping adds variety, as well as using sprinkles and edible glitter. I don't recommend dipping the whole pop in edible glitter, but a little sprinkle perks them up. You can also stripe the pops in a complimentary color of chocolate. Decorating the cake pops with fondant is another way to make your pops creative and fun. You can buy simple tools and molds at craft stores, and it is easy to do.

Check out all the cookbooks that are out there showing you how you can mold them and decorate them into all sorts of shapes. We have shaped them into animals and put hats and faces on them. If you have a theme for your party, I guarantee you can find a cake pop design that will go with it.

RED VELVET CAKE POPS

According to the internet, cake pops were first done by a cute blond lady whose professional name is Bakerella. When we were asked about them at Gabriel's, nothing would stop us until we had them in our case. The beauty of a cake pop is that decorating them is limited only by imagination, and they are the perfect bite of cake that you promise yourself is all you're going to eat! We make them in many different flavors at Gabriel's. Be careful. If folks find out you can make them, you'll be their best friend when they throw a party.

20 ounces of baked red velvet cake
   (4 1/2 to 5 cups)*
10 ounces cream cheese frosting

16 ounces white or red chocolate candy
   melts**
30 to 35 sucker sticks
Colored sprinkles

In a large bowl crumble the cake. Add the cream cheese frosting and blend with your hands (a mixer will over-blend this). Mix until you have a slightly moist "dough" that will hold the shape of a ball. If the mixture is too wet to hold together, add more cake. If it is too dry to hold together, add more cream cheese frosting.

Line a cookie sheet with parchment paper.

Use a size 40 scoop (sometimes labelled a "mini" in the grocery) to scoop the mixture into balls and place them on the pan.

Place the pan in the freezer for 20 minutes until the pops are firm and cold but not frozen.***

While the pops are chilling, melt the chocolate in the microwave in 10- to 15-second intervals at full power, stirring between intervals, or melt in a double boiler over simmering water.

Once the balls are cold and firm, roll each ball in your hands so that they are evenly round and smooth.

  * Your final result is not going to be any better than the cake you begin with. When baking a cake for an occasion, double your recipe or half again and store the extra layers in the freezer for making pops. Or bake your cake layers and frosting a day or so ahead of assembling your pops.
 ** Available at hobby stores. Almond bark can be purchased from grocery stores and is an acceptable substitute. Chocolate chips really don't work well.
*** The chocolate coating will crack if it is dipped when the cake is frozen. Should they freeze, let them sit out for a few minutes before you dip them.

Dip $^1/_4$ to $^1/_2$ inch of one end of the stick into the melted chocolate and press about half way into the ball.

If the pops have warmed up while out of the freezer, pop them back in until they're stiff again, but not frozen.

Dip the pops into the chocolate, completely covering the pop. Set them back on the parchment. Dust with sprinkles while the chocolate is still soft.

Makes 30 to 35 pops.

PLAYING IN THE KITCHEN

▶ Double Fudge Pops

20 ounces double fudge cake
7 ounces chocolate buttercream frosting

16 ounces semisweet chocolate melts
30 to 35 sucker sticks

Prepare according to Red Velvet Cake Pops recipe.

Makes 30 to 35 pops.

▶ Strawberry Pops

20 ounces fresh strawberry cake
5 ounces vanilla buttercream frosting
2 ounces strawberry jam

2 drops strawberry flavoring, optional
16 ounces white chocolate melts
30 to 35 sucker sticks

Prepare according to Red Velvet Cake Pops recipe, adding the jam and strawberry flavoring as you are combining the buttercream and cake.

Makes 30 to 35 pops.

FORT VALLEY PEACH COBBLER

Fort Valley, Georgia, is just one of the peach capitals of the South. Each peach-growing region claims the title. The family of my friend Sally Rhoden uses this recipe for a quick cobbler "fix." Sally's son, Mitch, recommends serving this cobbler warm with vanilla ice cream. I concur with Mitch!

3/4 cup all-purpose flour
2 cups sugar, divided
2 teaspoons baking powder
3/4 cup milk

Dash of salt
6 tablespoons butter
2 cups fresh peaches, peeled and sliced*

Preheat the oven to 350 degrees.

In a large bowl combine the flour, 1 cup of sugar, baking powder, milk, and salt. Stir to make a loose batter.

In a 2-quart casserole dish, melt the butter in the preheating oven. In a medium bowl, toss the peaches with the remaining 1 cup of sugar.

Carefully remove the dish from the oven when the butter is melted and pour the batter into the dish. Pour the peach mixture over the batter. Do not stir the peaches into the batter.

Bake for 1 hour or until brown and bubbly.

Makes 10 to 12 servings.

---

* I think canned, drained peaches will work in a pinch, but never substitute canned when you can get fresh. If you use frozen peaches, let them thaw and drain on a rack over a cookie sheet before you measure the two cups. They will shrink in volume a lot.

COCONUT CREAM PIE

This pie is the darling of desserts at the Gary Bonds Sunday school Christmas party (my class since 1972). Fellow class member Dot Downing makes this pie and agreed to share the recipe with me. Folks line up for Dot's pie before they help their plates to anything else. She makes two pies each year, and there are fifty to sixty folks attending, so you can imagine the mad scramble.

3/4 cup plus 6 tablespoons sugar, divided
1/3 cup all-purpose flour or 3 tablespoons
   cornstarch
1/4 teaspoon salt
2 cups milk
6 large eggs, separated
2 tablespoons butter

1 1/2 teaspoons vanilla extract, divided
1 1/3 cups flaked coconut, divided
1 refrigerated piecrust, baked according
   to package directions, or 1 (9-inch)
   deep-dish homemade piecrust
1/4 teaspoon cream of tartar

In a saucepan over medium heat, combine the sugar, flour, and salt. Gradually whisk in the milk. Cook and stir constantly until the mixture boils and thickens. Cook for 2 minutes longer. Remove from the heat.

In a small bowl lightly beat the egg yolks. Stir a small amount of the hot mixture into the yolks and then pour the yolk mixture into the saucepan. Cook for 2 minutes, stirring constantly. Remove from the heat. Add the butter, vanilla, and 1 cup coconut. To prevent a crust from forming, put clear plastic wrap directly on top. Make sure the plastic wrap is touching the entire surface of the hot pudding. Cool to room temperature.

Pour into the piecrust.

Preheat oven to 350 degrees. In a large bowl beat the egg whites with the cream of tartar and vanilla in a stand mixer until soft peaks form. Gradually add the sugar and beat until stiff peaks form and all the sugar is dissolved. Spread on top of the pie, to the pastry. Sprinkle the remaining 1/3 cup coconut flakes over the meringue. Bake for 12 to 15 minutes, or until the meringue is golden. Cool. Store in the refrigerator.

Makes 6 to 8 servings.

CHOCOLATE PIE

The filling for this pie is a cooked custard. It's poured into a precooked piecrust and then topped with meringue. It's so easy, and it makes a gorgeous presentation! Semisweet chocolate lovers will love this one.

1 cup plus 1 tablespoon sugar, divided
1/4 cup plus 2 teaspoons cornstarch
1/4 cup cocoa powder
1/8 teaspoon salt
3 large eggs
3 cups whole milk

1 1/2 tablespoons butter
6 ounces semisweet chocolate chips
1 1/2 teaspoons vanilla extract
1 (9-inch) deep-dish piecrust, prebaked
1/4 teaspoon cream of tartar
1 tablespoon water

Preheat the oven to 350 degrees.

In a heavy saucepan combine 3/4 cup sugar, cornstarch, cocoa, and salt; whisk, combining well. Separate the yolks and whites of the eggs. In a medium bowl combine the egg yolks and milk. Save the egg whites for the meringue. Whisk the yolk mixture into the sugar mixture. Place the saucepan over medium heat and cook, stirring constantly with a wooden spoon. Be sure to stir all the way to the sides of the saucepan. Cook for 8 to 10 minutes until the mixture thickens and comes to a boil. Boil for 1 minute more, continuing to stir. Remove the pan from the heat and stir in the butter, chocolate chips, and vanilla. Pour the custard into the prebaked piecrust and immediately spread plastic wrap over the top of the custard, pressing out any air bubbles. This prevents a tough "skin" from forming on the top of the custard.

In the bowl of a stand mixer with a paddle attachment beat the egg whites, cream of tartar, and water until foamy. Add the remaining sugar 1 tablespoon at a time, beating after each addition. Continue beating until stiff peaks form.

Remove the plastic wrap from the custard and spread the whites over the top of the custard, spreading all the way to the edges of the crust to seal the top. Use a spatula to form peaks on top of the meringue.

Bake for 12 to 15 minutes or until the meringue is golden brown. Remove and let set for 30 to 45 minutes before serving. Refrigerate any leftovers.

Makes 8 to 10 servings.

Chocolate Pie (page 185)

EGG CUSTARD PIE

An old Southern favorite.

4 large eggs
2/3 cup sugar
2 2/3 cups whole milk
1 1/2 teaspoon vanilla extract

1/4 teaspoon salt
1 egg white
1/8 teaspoon nutmeg, optional
1 refrigerated piecrust*

Preheat the oven to 350 degrees.

Place the eggs and sugar in the large bowl of a stand mixer and beat until the sugar is dissolved. Add the milk, vanilla, and salt and combine well.

Prepare the piecrust according to the package directions and press into a 9-inch deep-dish pie plate. Brush the piecrust with a light coating of egg white to prevent the crust from being soggy. Place the pie plate on a cookie tray and carefully pour the custard into the crust.** Sprinkle the top lightly with the nutmeg. Bake for 10 to 12 minutes. Reduce the heat to 325 degrees and bake for another 50 minutes. Remove the pie when the center is a bit soft and jiggly.

Makes 6 to 8 servings.

NOTE: Baking this pie too long will make the custard watery.

* A store-bought piecrust can be used, but if time permits make a homemade crust. See recipe on page xx.
** The empty piecrust can be set on a pan on the oven shelf and filled from the mixing bowl so that you don't spill the filling out as you're carrying it to put into the oven. The filling doesn't rise while baking.

Lemon Icebox Pie

This pie was originally served in the Old Southern Tea Room in Vicksburg, Mississippi. There's only one word for this pie: delicious!

1 ¹/₂ cups vanilla wafer crumbs (about 28 wafers)
1 (14-ounce) can sweetened condensed milk

3 large eggs, separated
Juice of 3 large lemons
6 tablespoons sugar

Preheat the oven to 350 degrees. Butter a 9-inch pie plate.*

Line the bottom and sides of the pie plate with the vanilla wafer crumbs. In a medium bowl combine the condensed milk, egg yolks, and lemon juice. Whisk to combine. Pour into the pie plate.

Place the egg whites in the bowl of a stand mixer and beat until foamy. Add the sugar 1 tablespoon at a time and beat until stiff peaks form. Spread over the lemon mixture.

Bake about 12 minutes, or until the meringue is light golden brown. Chill before serving.

Makes 6 to 8 servings.

* Using butter is a must. The butter causes the vanilla wafers to adhere to the sides of the pie plate.

Lemon Icebox Pie (page 189)

PIECRUSTS

When I began this cookbook, I realized I didn't have a vivid memory of "scratch" piecrusts being made. I must admit that when I did my own pie baking at home, I was more likely to run to the grocery store for a premade crust. So I set out in pursuit of the very best "scratch" piecrust so I could share the recipe with you. I collected recipes and began to bake. I made piecrusts that were all butter, all shortening, and a combination of shortening and butter. I compelled the pastry chefs at Gabriel's to taste them all and give me their opinion. I ate so much piecrust in ten days I thought I never wanted to make or eat another one. I'm sure I'll get over that.

After much research but never quite being able to settle on a favorite, several people came to my rescue. One was Anna McNabb, a chef at Gabriel's. Anna is British, a trained chef, and makes the most exquisite gum paste flowers you have ever laid your eyes on. I'll put her flowers on one of our cakes up beside Sylvia Weinstock's any day. Anna has shared her piecrust recipe with me. She says in forty years it has never failed her. You can find it on page 196.

Susan Johnson, now a neighbor and also a contributor of several recipes in *Second Helpings*, connected me with her friend Carole Lang. When Susan, who is a wonderful cook and baker, stated that Carole is the best baker she knows, she really got my attention. Carole attributes the best piecrust recipe to her mother, Jean Perry. Her recipe is on page 193.

Make them both. I'm not saying which is my favorite. I'll let you all decide.

Now that I have made and tasted these wonderful piecrusts, I am a convert. Will I ever pull another premade piecrust off the grocery store shelf? Probably, but only in a pinch, and with a great deal of remorse as to what I'll be missing.

PIECRUST

This is the recipe Jean Perry's daughter Carole Lang shared with me via my friend Susan Johnson. Thanks, Jean and Carole!

2 1/2 cups all-purpose flour, plus more for
    dusting the board
1 1/2 teaspoons sugar
1 teaspoon salt

1/2 cup (1 stick) cold butter, cut into
    cubes
1/2 cup lard or vegetable shortening,
    frozen
5 tablespoons cold water

Put the flour, sugar, and salt into a food processor.* Pulse a couple of times to thoroughly combine. Add the butter and lard and pulse until the ingredients look like coarse bread crumbs. Pea-size pieces of butter are desirable and will promote a flaky crust. Add the cold water and pulse until the mixture comes together, forming a dough. Immediately stop and take the dough out of the bowl of the food processor and place on a floured surface. Knead a couple of times but do not over-knead. Divide the dough in half. Shape each piece into a slightly flattened disk. Wrap in plastic wrap and refrigerate for an hour or up to 3 days before rolling out.

When ready to bake, preheat oven to 350 degrees.

Remove the disk from the refrigerator and let sit at room temperature to allow it to soften a bit. Place on a lightly floured surface and, with a floured rolling pin, roll into a circle 2 inches larger than the pie pan. As you are rolling, gently lift and turn the dough to be sure it's not sticking to the surface. If it begins to stick, sprinkle more flour onto the board. Roll the dough to about 1/8-inch thickness. Carefully drape one edge of the dough over the rolling pin and roll the remaining dough over the pin, using the pin to move the dough to the pie pan. Gently press the pie dough into the pan so that it lines the bottom and sides. Trim the dough, leaving about 1/2 inch of pastry over the edge of the pan.

For a single prebaked crust: Tuck the overhanging underneath itself along the edge of the pie pan. Use your fingers to pinch or crimp the edge of the piecrust or use the tines of a fork to shape the edge. Freeze the crust for at least 30 minutes to prevent shrinkage. Line the crust with foil and fill with dried beans, uncooked rice, or pie weights to hold the crust in shape while you're prebaking. Bake about 20 minutes and remove the weights. Use a fork to prick a few holes in the bottom of the crust and return to the oven for about 10 more minutes, baking until a golden color.

Makes pastry for 2 single-crust pies or 1 double-crust pie.

* A food processor is not required to make pie dough. It can just as easily be made using a bowl and a pastry cutter.

ANNA'S PIE CRUST FOR SWEET OR SAVORY

Anna McNabb currently works in the savory part of our kitchen. She is a chef, a baker, has been a restaurant owner, and hand makes the most beautiful, botanically correct gum paste flowers for cake decorating. Her own estimate is that she has made thousands of pie crusts in her days in the kitchen.

2 cups all-purpose flour, plus more for rolling
Pinch of sea salt
Pinch of sugar
1/2 cup (1 stick) unsalted butter, cut into cubes and refrigerated

3 tablespoons vegetable shortening, cut into cubes and refrigerated
5 tablespoons ice cold water

Spoon the flour, salt, and sugar into the bowl of a food processor. Pulse a couple of times to thoroughly combine. Add the butter and vegetable shortening and pulse until the mixture looks like coarse bread crumbs. Pea-size pieces of butter are desirable and will promote a flaky crust. Add the ice water and pulse until the mixture comes together forming a dough. Immediately stop and take the dough out of the processor and place on a floured surface. Knead a couple of times but do not over-knead. Shape the mixture into a large, flat disk 4 to 5 inches in diameter. Wrap in plastic wrap and refrigerate for 30 minutes and up to 2 days before rolling out. The dough can be frozen and thawed in the refrigerator before rolling out.

When ready to roll, remove the disk from the refrigerator and let it sit at room temperature for 10 to 15 minutes, until it is soft enough to roll. Place on a lightly floured surface and use a floured rolling pin to roll into an 11- or 12-inch circle (it should be about 2 inches larger than a pie pan). As you are rolling, gently lift and turn the dough to be sure it's not sticking to the surface. If it sticks, sprinkle more flour onto the rolling surface. Roll to about 1/8 inch thick. Carefully drape one edge of the crust over the rolling pin and loosely roll the crust over the pin, using the pin to move the crust to the pie pan. Gently press the pie dough down so that it lines the bottom and sides of the plate. Trim the dough to within 1/2 inch of the edge of the pan.

For a single-crust prebaked and then filled pie: Freeze the crust for at least 30 minutes to prevent shrinkage. Preheat the oven to 425 degrees. Line the crust with aluminum foil and fill with dried beans, uncooked rice, or pie weights to hold in the crust's shape while you're prebaking. Bake about 15 minutes. Remove the weights and foil. Use a fork to prick a few holes in the bottom of the crust and return it to the oven for about 10 more minutes. Bake until the crust is golden.

Makes 2 (9-inch) deep-dish piecrusts

SNICKERDOODLES

Cinnamon and sugar combine to make the snickerdoodle one of the best-selling cookies we bake at Gabriel's. These are great cookies for just a little bit of sweetness after a meal or with a glass of cold milk. We use a large scoop at Gabriel's to make a 3- to 4-inch cookie and also use a small scoop to make what we call a "silver dollar" cookie. I thought the children would find them the perfect size, but it's the adults who always ask if we're sure we put in their two complimentary silver dollars with their to-go order. This recipe makes a large quantity, but the dough can be broken into two or three quantities and frozen for later use. Just thaw for several hours in the refrigerator before scooping. Better yet, scoop the dough, freeze on a cookie sheet, then store in freezer bags and remove and thaw the quantity you want to bake.

1 1/4 cups (2 1/2 sticks) butter, softened
1 1/4 cups vegetable oil
2 3/4 cups white sugar, divided
2 1/2 cups powdered sugar
3 large eggs
2 teaspoons vanilla extract

6 1/4 cups all-purpose flour
2 teaspoons plus 1/4 teaspoon baking soda
2 teaspoons cream of tartar
3/4 teaspoon salt
2 tablespoons ground cinnamon

Place the butter and oil in the bowl of a stand mixer and combine on low speed for 1 minute. Scrape down the sides of the bowl and the paddle. Increase the speed to medium and mix for 2 to 5 minutes. The mixture should be smooth with no lumps of butter.

In a medium bowl sift the 1 1/4 cups white sugar and the powdered sugar together. Add all at once into the butter mixture and mix on low for 5 minutes.

Add the eggs and vanilla to the creamed mixture and mix on low for 5 minutes. Scrape down the sides of the bowl and the paddle. Increase the speed to medium and mix for another 5 minutes.

Sift the flour into a large bowl. Add the baking soda, cream of tartar, and salt. Stir to combine. Add a third of the flour mixture to the creamed mixture and mix on low to combine. Add the remaining flour mixture in two batches, mixing on low after each addition. Scrape down the sides of the bowl and the paddle and mix on low for 1 more minute.

Move the cookie dough to an appropriate storage container and place in the refrigerator to chill before scooping, at least 2 hours.

Preheat the oven to 350 degrees. Line a cookie sheet with parchment paper.

Combine the remaining 1 $1/2$ cups sugar and cinnamon in a shallow dish.

Scoop the dough with a medium scoop and roll it in the cinnamon-sugar mixture. Place the dough on the cookie sheet 3 to 4 inches apart. Bake for 8 minutes, turn, and bake for 8 more minutes. The cookies are done when they just begin to brown on the edges.

Makes 25 to 28 cookies.

NOTE: This recipe can also be used to make sugar cookies. Just roll the dough in colored sanding sugar before baking.

TIP: Using a cookie scoop gives you a more consistent cookie size. Scoops can be found in most large grocery stores and in kitchen specialty stores.

Russian Tea Cakes aka Mexican Wedding Cookies aka Pecan Sandies

This cookie/tea cake practically melts in your mouth. The butter and pecan flavors come together and are then rolled in powdered sugar while still warm. My grandmother made them for us and called them pecan sandies.

1 cup (2 sticks) butter, softened
3 cups powdered sugar, divided
1 teaspoon vanilla extract

2 1/4 cups all-purpose flour
1/4 teaspoon salt
3/4 cup pecans, chopped

Preheat the oven to 325 degrees. Line a cookie sheet with parchment paper.

Place the butter and 3/4 cup of powdered sugar in a large bowl of a stand mixer and mix. Add the vanilla and mix to combine.

Sift the flour into a medium bowl and stir in the salt to combine. With the mixer running, slowly add the flour mixture to the butter mixture and combine until the flour is just incorporated. Add the pecans and stir with a spatula.

With a small scoop, portion out the dough and roll into balls. Place on the cookie sheet and bake for 10 to 12 minutes. Check the cookies after 10 minutes. If the bottoms are golden brown, remove them from the oven and cool momentarily.

Pour the remaining 2 1/4 cups of powdered sugar in a medium bowl. Toss the warm cookies in the sugar to completely cover. Use a fork or slotted spoon to remove the cookies. Place in a single layer on a parchment paper–lined cookie sheet to cool.

Store in an airtight container for 4–5 days or freeze for up to 1 month. If frozen, remove from the freezer, separate, and thaw uncovered.

Makes 3 dozen cookies.

PUMPKIN CAKE

This is a third-generation recipe from a customer at Gabriel's. Kellie True's grandmother Helen West first made it for Kellie's family as a part of a picnic lunch she prepared for a road trip to her east Tennessee home. They couldn't stop talking about it. Kellie's mom baked it for her, and now Kellie bakes it for her daughters. Her girls can't wait for the Thanksgiving meal and eat a piece while it's still warm just out of the oven. It's a part of the cherished memories they have of their great-grandmother and continues to be a part of their family celebrations.

3 cups self-rising flour
2 cups sugar
1 1/4 teaspoons cinnamon
1 cup vegetable oil

4 large eggs
2 2/3 cups pumpkin pie filling or mix*
1 (12-ounce) bag semisweet chocolate
chips

Set the oven rack on the next to the last shelf from the bottom and preheat the oven to 350 degrees. Grease a 10-inch tube pan.

In a large bowl combine the flour, sugar, and cinnamon and stir to evenly distribute. Add the oil, eggs, and pie filling.

Use a hand mixer to beat on medium speed until flour mixture is incorporated.

Fold in the chocolate chips and pour into the tube pan. Bake for 60 minutes or until a cake tester inserted near the center comes out clean. Let cool in the pan for 10 minutes, then turn out onto a rack to cool completely.

Makes 12 to 14 servings.

* Make sure the can reads pie filling or pie mix. Manufacturers no longer make the exact can size needed for this recipe. About three-quarters of a large can will ensure a delicious cake.

It doesn't get any
sweeter than this

SWEET POTATO PIE

Dorothy Woodruff is a great cook and hostess. Dorothy and her parents emigrated from England when Dorothy was four. They settled in Detroit and lived there through her teenage years. Marietta got lucky when she married a Southerner. She cooks for her family and entertains with some great Southern recipes. Sweet potato pie is one of them.

2 large sweet potatoes
1/4 cup vegetable oil
3/4 cup (1 1/4 sticks) butter
1 3/4 cups sugar
1 1/4 teaspoons vanilla extract

3 large eggs
1/2 cup evaporated milk
Dash of lemon juice
1 cup canned, flake coconut, optional
1 refrigerated piecrust*

Preheat the oven to 350 degrees.

Wash the sweet potatoes and brush the skins with a bit of vegetable oil. Bake for 1 hour. Potatoes are done when they are soft when squeezed.

Peel the potatoes when cool enough to handle and place in a large bowl. Add the butter and beat well with an hand mixer. Let the mixture cool. Add the sugar, vanilla, eggs, and milk. Beat well. Add the lemon juice and coconut if desired.

Prepare the piecrust according to the package directions and press into a 9-inch pie pan. Pour the potato filling into the piecrust and bake until set, 50 to 60 minutes. The center may still be a bit soft and jiggly but not liquid. A knife inserted an inch or so from the crust should come out clean.

Makes 8 servings.

* A store-bought piecrust can be used, but if time permits make a homemade crust. See recipes on pages 193 or 196.

Sweet Potato Pie (page 203)

SAND TARTS

My friend Liz Bergin Cole has made this little cookie for me many times now. After her mom's death, Liz became the designated baker of these sand tarts for her dad, Jack Bergin. He lived in their hometown of Ocean Springs, Mississippi, and she was in Marietta, so she cut them to fit in a tennis ball can and mailed them to him. These cookies are delicious at an afternoon tea, especially with the addition of lavender. With or without lavender, a coffee and this little cookie is the perfect end to a meal.

2 cups all-purpose flour
1 1/2 teaspoons baking powder
1/2 cup (1 stick) butter, softened

1 cup sugar
1 large egg, slightly beaten

Preheat the oven to 375 degrees.

Sift the flour into a medium bowl. Add the baking powder and combine.

In a medium bowl cream the butter using a hand mixer. Add the sugar and continue to mix until the mixture becomes light and fluffy.

Add the egg to the sugar mixture and mix to incorporate. Add the flour mixture and mix until well blended.

Turn the dough out onto a floured surface and roll to 1/8-inch thick. Use a small cookie cutter and place the dough on ungreased cookie sheets. Bake for 10 minutes.*

Makes about 4 dozen small cookies.

PLAYING IN THE KITCHEN: Liz was recently inspired by Jodi Rhoden, owner of Short Street Bakery in Asheville, North Carolina, to adapt this family recipe to make Lavender Tea Cakes. Simply add 1/2 to 1 teaspoon culinary lavender flowers with the flour mixture.

* If you prefer crispier cookies, bake at 275 degrees until brown, about 15 minutes.

STRAWBERRY SHORTCAKE CAKE

The Ausburn-Teague family cookbook calls this the "Lazy Susan Cake" because it's the easiest cake you'll ever make, and it's low fat. When we tested this in the bakery at Gabriel's, we topped it with fresh whipped cream. The cake is soft and soaks up the strawberry juice, and it's just the right amount of sweet to let the berries shine. My fork slid right into that little cake, and when I popped it into my mouth, it transported me to Sunday lunch at Big Mama's. I can think of few things more Southern than Big Mama, Sunday lunch, and strawberry shortcake.

3 (1-pound) cartons fresh strawberries, washed, hulled, and sliced
3/4 cup sugar or to taste for sprinkling over sliced berries
1/2 cup milk
1 tablespoon butter
2 large eggs

1 cup sugar
1 teaspoon vanilla extract
1 cup sifted all-purpose flour
1 teaspoon baking powder
1/4 teaspoon salt
2 to 3 cups heavy cream, whipped*
1/4 to 1/3 cup powdered sugar

Six to 8 hours before serving the shortcake, put the strawberries in a large bowl and sprinkle with the sugar. Cover and refrigerate. A sweet strawberry juice will accumulate in the bowl.**

Preheat the oven to 350 degrees. Grease and flour an 8 x 8-inch baking pan.

Pour the milk into a small saucepan over medium-low heat. Add the butter and warm. When the butter melts, remove the pan from the heat.

In a stand mixer with a paddle attachment, beat the eggs until they begin to thicken. Add the sugar and vanilla and beat well.

In a small bowl stir together the flour, baking powder, and salt. Add to the creamed mixture and mix on low. With the motor running on low, add the warm milk mixture and mix to combine.

Pour into the baking pan and bake for 25 to 30 minutes until a cake tester inserted into the middle of the cake comes out clean.

Let cool in the pan 10 minutes and turn out onto wire rack to cool.

While the cake is cooling, pour the cream into a large, chilled bowl and begin to slowly whip the cream with an electric mixer. If you like the cream slightly sweet, slowly sprinkle $^1/4$ to $^1/3$ cup powdered sugar over the cream. Increase the speed to medium-high and whip until the cream will hold a soft peak.

To assemble the shortcakes, cut the cake into 9 equal pieces. Slice each piece horizontally and place the bottom pieces on serving plates. Spoon the berries and juice over the bottom pieces. Place the top slices off center of the berries and spoon more berries and juice over the top pieces. Top with fresh whipped cream. Stand one strawberry slice up on top of whipped cream.

Makes 8 to 10 servings.

---

* You can substitute canned or frozen whipped cream, but I highly recommend freshly whipped cream for this dessert.
** This process of slicing fruit and sprinkling with sugar is called macerating. The sugar causes the fruit to "give up" its natural juices and lets the fruit soak in it. This maceration process can be done with sugar alone or with an alcohol, such as Gran Marnier or a wine, or other juices for the addition of another flavor.

POUND CAKE

Any Southern cook who's serious about her desserts has a "go to" pound cake recipe. It's one of the first foods to show up at a potluck dinner or a funeral, and they almost always sell out at Gabriel's. They are so versatile, and the ingredients are usually on hand if you're baking at home. The recipe I am sharing with you is a bit different from the one we bake at the store. While doing physical therapy for my second knee replacement, one of my physical therapists said, "My mama makes the best pound cake you'll ever eat." That really got my attention and I, of course, asked for the recipe. Her mom, Jane Hecht, of Columbus, Georgia, shared it with me along with jars of her pickled squash, spiced peaches, and pepper jelly. If you can grow it, I believe Jane preserves it! Waste doesn't seem to be in her vocabulary, evidenced by all the uses she has for her pound cake. First she serves slices of the cake. Any leftovers? Just butter and toast it. Then she serves it with sugared strawberries or peaches. Still have some pound cake left? Put it in a trifle, or crumble it and use it as the bottom of a cheesecake. After baking and eating Jane's version of a pound cake, I doubt any of her cake gets to the base of a cheesecake!

....

2 cups (4 sticks) salted butter, softened	4 cups sifted cake flour
3 1/2 cups sugar	1 cup heavy whipping cream
2 cups eggs* (about 7 or 8, whisked)	1 to 1 1/2 teaspoons vanilla

....

Do not preheat the oven.

Grease and flour a 10-inch tube pan or use a baking spray and flour the pan.

In a large bowl beat the butter and sugar with a stand mixer until soft and creamy. Scrape down the sides and bottom several times. Add the eggs, 1/4 cup at a time, and beat well after each addition. Scrape down the bowl frequently. Alternately, add the flour and the whipping cream, beginning and ending with the flour, scraping down the sides of the bowl. Add the vanilla and mix just until the last of the flour is combined.

Pour batter into prepared pan and tap the pan on the counter top several times to even out and settle the batter. Using a table knife, swirl through the batter to release any air bubbles. Place the pan on the bottom rack of a cold oven. Take out the top rack of the oven as the cake will rise very high in the pan when baking.

Turn the oven to 325 degrees and bake for 1 hour and 15 minutes without opening the oven door. Test for doneness by inserting a cake tester into the cake.

It should come out moist but without wet batter on it. If necessary, bake for another 5 to 15 minutes.

The cake will rise up high and then fall back a little. As soon as you test the cake and see that it's done, use a rubber spatula and push the edge of the cake back inside the edge of the pan to keep from losing that delicious crust when the cake settles back down.

Set the cake on a rack to cool. It will continue to cook a bit as it cools down. Cool for 10 to 15 minutes in the pan and turn out onto a plate.

Makes 12 to 14 servings.

* Jane prefers brown eggs.

Caramel Apple Bread Pudding

Jeffry Webb, our pastry chef at Gabriel's, introduced us to this awesome dessert. I have never had anyone try it that didn't love it!

17 to 18 ounces challah bread, cut into
   1-inch cubes
7 large eggs
2 1/4 cups granulated sugar, divided
2 1/2 teaspoons ground cinnamon
2 teaspoons ground nutmeg
1 quart plus 4 ounces heavy cream,
   divided

2 teaspoons vanilla extract
3 tablespoons butter
4 1/2 to 5 Granny Smith apples, peeled,
   cored, and sliced
1/2 cup caramel sauce
Vanilla ice cream for serving
Fresh mint for garnish

Preheat the oven to 225 degrees.

Place the bread cubes on a cookie sheet and toast for about 20 minutes. Remove from the oven and put into a large bowl.

Increase the oven to 375 degrees. Spray a 9 x 13-inch casserole dish generously with nonstick cooking spray.

In a large bowl whisk the eggs.

In a large saucepan combine the 1 3/4 cups sugar, cinnamon, and nutmeg. Whisk to combine. Add 1 1/4 cups cream and vanilla and bring to a boil over medium heat.

Once the mixture is hot, ladle a small amount into the eggs and whisk to keep the eggs from curdling. When tempered add all of cream to the eggs and set aside.

In a skillet over medium heat melt the butter and the remaining 1/2 cup sugar. Add the apples and sauté until they are softened a bit. Add the apples to the bread and mix thoroughly.

Pour the cream mixture over the bread and let soak an hour or until the bread is completely submerged. You may have to use the back of a spoon to press the bread down into the cream mixture, until it begins to soak in.

Spread the mixture into the casserole dish. Place the dish in a roasting pan and pour hot water into the roasting pan about halfway up the side of the smaller baking dish to create a water bath. Bake 40 minutes or until puffed and golden and a toothpick inserted in the center comes out clean. Remove the dish from the water bath and set on a wire rack to cool.

Drizzle with the caramel sauce while the pudding is still warm. Serve warm or room temperature with vanilla ice cream and a sprig of fresh mint.

Makes 18 (2 x 3-inch) pieces.

Chocolate Brownies

My friend Lynda Ausburn's family has joyful and comforting memories of these delicious brownies made by her mom, Mrs. Caroline Teague. This is a family-size recipe; cut it in half for a smaller crowd.

Brownies
1/2 teaspoon salt
2 1/4 cups self-rising flour
3 cups sugar
3 heaping tablespoons cocoa
6 large eggs
1 cup plus 2 tablespoons (2 1/4 sticks)
    butter, melted
1 tablespoon vanilla extract
1 1/2 cups pecans, chopped

Frosting
1 cup (2 sticks) butter
7 3/4 cup plus 2 tablespoons milk
1/2 cup cocoa powder
2 pounds powdered sugar, sifted
2 teaspoons vanilla extract

To make the brownies: Preheat the oven to 350 degrees. Grease two 9 x 13-inch baking pans.

In a medium bowl combine salt, flour, sugar, and cocoa together. Place the eggs, melted butter, and vanilla in the bowl of a stand mixer. Beat to combine. Mix in the flour mixture and pecans until just incorporated. Do not overmix. Pour the batter into the pan and bake for 20 to 25 minutes. The brownies are ready when a cake tester (or toothpick) comes out clean. Place on a wire rack to cool while you make the frosting.

To make the frosting: Place a large saucepan over high heat and add the butter, milk, and cocoa powder. Whisk and bring to a boil. This will happen quickly, so watch carefully. Remove the pan from the heat and whisk in the powdered sugar and the vanilla. Mix until the sugar is completely combined. Pour and spread over the cooled brownies while the frosting is still warm. Let cool until the frosting forms a "crust" and loses its sheen before cutting.

Makes 64 (2 x 1/2-inch) brownies.

NOTE: Lynda makes her frosting from memory, but I have to have a written one, so I'm sharing Gabriel's recipe with you with Lynda's approval.

ICE CREAM

When I was growing up, Friday night dinners in Albany with my Aunt Mabel Bass ended with peach ice cream dipped right out of the churn. A wooden bucket outfitted with a mechanism that latched on the bucket and spun a metal cylinder with a paddle inside "churned" the cream to the proper consistency. Also on hand were extra bags of ice to pack around the metal container while the ice cream was churning, rock salt to sprinkle over the ice to slow the melting of the ice in the hot, humid weather, and strong-armed men to hand crank the churn. When arms had been exhausted, we would pack more ice around the container, sprinkle a little more salt, and spread newspapers over the top of the churn while the ice cream set up. As a child that was the hardest time for me . . . waiting, knowing that wonderful soft, cold peach cream was just sitting in that wooden bucket.

Eventually, electric ice-cream freezers came on the market and we had homemade ice cream a little more often. And you can too. Most popular countertop ice-cream makers yield about 2 quarts as opposed to the 4 to 5 quarts of old. This recipe is written for the 2-quart countertop size currently on the market. I have had the most success with this type when I planned ahead and put the empty bowl in the freezer for 18 to 24 hours before filling. My friend and chef Debbie Willyard stores her empty bowl in the freezer . . . it's always ready!

HOMEMADE VANILLA ICE CREAM

Homemade ice cream is as Southern as fried chicken, biscuits, and gravy. When making homemade ice cream from a cooked custard base, it's a good idea to make the custard the day before you plan to serve the ice cream and store it in the refrigerator overnight to chill.

1 vanilla bean*
2 1/2 cups whole milk
2 2/3 cups heavy cream

10 egg yolks
1 3/4 cups sugar

Four to 6 hours before you plan to churn your ice cream, split the vanilla bean lengthwise and use the tip of a sharp knife to scrape out the seeds. Place the vanilla bean and seeds in a medium saucepan along with the milk and the cream. Place the saucepan over medium heat and heat the milk until hot but not boiling. Remove the pan from the heat and allow the vanilla to infuse the milk for 30 minutes. In a medium bowl mix the egg yolks and sugar.

Remove the vanilla bean** from the milk.

Whisk the infused milk into the yolk mixture. When fully blended, set aside while you wash and dry the saucepan you used to infuse the milk.

Return the milk and egg mixture to the clean saucepan and cook over medium-low heat, stirring constantly, until the custard has thickened sufficiently to coat the back of a wooden spoon. Don't allow the mixture to boil or it will curdle.

Strain the mixture into a bowl or a 9 x 13-inch casserole dish if you need it to cool quickly. Cool the mixture only slightly before covering with plastic wrap gently pressed directly against the surface of the custard to prevent a film from forming. Refrigerate until chilled through, 4 to 6 hours.

When ready to churn, pour the custard into the bowl of a 2-quart ice-cream maker and follow the manufacturer's directions for ice-cream churning.

Makes 2 quarts.

* If you don't have a vanilla bean, use 2 teaspoons vanilla extract, but wait to add it to the custard after you have removed the pan from the heat.
** Rinse and lay the bean aside to dry, then reuse by adding the bean to a container of sugar to infuse the sugar.

Coconut Cream Key West Lime Sorbet with Homemade Graham Cracker Crust Chunks

Jason Cyr has become the homemade ice-cream guru of his somewhat newly married-into Southern family. As a member of the now Cyr–McEachern–Teh–Dunaway family, he has put the pressure on himself to become the family's official flavor developer of homemade ice cream. He has now gone where no other family member has tread and is doing a darn good job! He declares this to be one of the most favored recipes among his friends and family. It's great for the summertime as it combines the tartness of the key lime juice with the smooth chunks of coconut fat and the crunch of the graham cracker crust.

Homemade Graham Cracker Crust

1/3 cup butter*
1 1/4 cups graham cracker crumbs

1/4 cup sugar*

Preheat the oven to 350 degrees.

Melt the butter in a medium glass bowl. Add the graham cracker crumbs and sugar to the bowl and stir until completely incorporated. Press the graham cracker mixture firmly into a 9-inch pie plate and bake for 8 to 10 minutes. Cool overnight so it gets nice and crunchy. Break into medium chunks when ready to use in the sorbet or store in a plastic bag or container and freeze for future use.

Sorbet

2 (15-ounce) cans cream of coconut (full fat)
1 1/2 cups water

1 cup lime juice (such as Nellie & Joe's Famous Key West Lime Juice)

Wisk the cream of coconut, water, and lime juice in a large bowl. Refrigerate this mixture for at least 12 hours. The fat will congeal into absolutely amazing coconut fat chunks when put into the ice-cream maker.

Place the mixture in a 2-quart ice-cream maker and process for 20 to 25 minutes, until it reaches the consistency of soft serve. Add the graham cracker crust chunks for the last 2 minutes of churning. Let the container set in the freezer for 4 to 6 hours.

Makes 2 quarts.

* Jason uses Kerrygold butter and organic cane sugar because he prefers the flavors.

Vanilla Ice Cream No-Cook Style

Homemade and no cooking required! Janet Byington of Rome has been generous with her family recipes, and all of us ice-cream lovers are grateful. This vanilla ice cream is delicious on its own, and it will give you a good, easy starting point for developing your family's favorite flavor. I have cut Janet's original recipe in half to fit into my 2-quart countertop ice-cream maker. Just double it for the gallon-size freezer and have a box of rock salt on hand to use with churns requiring ice.

1 1/2 cups sugar
1 1/2 teaspoons vanilla extract
Pinch of salt

2 cups whipping cream
3 3/4 cups whole milk

In a large bowl whisk together the sugar, vanilla, salt, whipping cream, and milk, combining well. Pour into the ice-cream freezer and process according to manufacturer's directions.

Store the ice cream in the freezer for at least 2 hours before serving or serve it immediately for soft serve.

Makes 2 quarts.

Homemade Peach Ice Cream

I love ice cream in the summer and in the winter; it doesn't really matter what the temperature is outside. As a Southerner, though, probably no dessert other than cold watermelon symbolizes a summer in the South more than homemade peach ice cream. I grew up in Georgia peach country, and my family was a frequent shopper at the farmers' market. When the peaches, corn, butter beans, peas, and green beans came in, we bought them all by the bushel. We enjoyed the vegetables fresh during the season, but the main objective was to freeze quarts of them to enjoy during the winter. My favorite was, of course, the peach ice cream, always and only made from fresh peaches. I never could convince Daddy to pull out the ice-cream freezer in the winter, even when we still had frozen peaches. But these days I have my own ice-cream churn and I can have ice cream anytime I want. And you can too. The following is my adaption of Tom McEachern's no-cook custard recipe in Cooking in the South.

3 medium peaches, peeled, pitted, cut into 1/2-inch pieces (about 2 cups)
1/2 teaspoon lemon juice
Pinch of salt

1/4 cup sugar
1 recipe Vanilla Ice Cream No-Cook Style (page 216)*

In a medium bowl combine the peaches, lemon juice, salt, and sugar. Cover and allow to sit on the counter for 1 hour.

In a medium saucepan heat the softened peaches and liquid over medium-high heat, stirring until the peaches are tender and the flesh is broken down. Return the peaches to the bowl, cover, and place in the refrigerator to chill thoroughly.

Add the peaches to the vanilla ice cream during the last 3 to 4 minutes of churning. Freeze for up to 2 hours before serving.

Makes 2 quarts.

* When preparing the vanilla ice cream that you plan to add fruit to, reduce the amount of milk used by the same amount of fruit you are adding. For example, if you add 1 1/2 cups of peaches, reduce the amount of milk from 3 3/4 cups to 2 1/4 cups or your churn will overflow when you add the peaches.

PLAYING IN THE KITCHEN: This ice cream is so delicious. I can think of so many ways to take advantage of its flavor by adding the following during the last two minutes of churning:

$^{1}/_{2}$ to 1 cup blueberries

1 to 2 cups fresh peaches

1 to 2 cups small chunks of pound cake

LEMON ICE CREAM

My friend Janet Byington from Rome, Georgia, shared a couple of her mother's and grandmother's recipes. These are the kind of recipes I cherish someone sharing. I fear that so many family recipes are not going to be written down or passed down to the next generation. I have fun memories of visiting the ice-cream company close to my childhood home in downtown Macon. My favorite flavor was lemon custard. Yum! Refreshing, cold, and tart but sweet—what relief on a hot summer Sunday afternoon or evening. Janet's recipe reminds me of that custard. This recipe is for a 4-quart freezer. If you use a 2-quart electric countertop one, just cut this recipe in half.

3 1/2 cups sugar
6 lemons, divided
1 teaspoon salt
2 teaspoons lemon zest

1 quart heavy whipping cream
2 quarts whole milk
Rock salt or ice cream salt

In a large bowl mix the sugar and the juice of only 4 lemons, salt, and zest. Stir in the cream and milk.

Very thinly slice the remaining 2 lemons. Cut the slices into quarters and add to the milk mixture.

Pour into the ice-cream maker and process according to the manufacturer's directions. Be sure to use salt in the freezer to freeze the ice cream if you are using an old-fashioned ice-cream freezer.

Makes 4 quarts.

Milk Chocolate and Salt-Covered Bacon Ice Cream

Jason Cyr, new to the South and husband of my friend Claire Dunaway Cyr, has taken on the task (and loves it) of introducing new-to-the-South, homemade ice-cream flavors. This recipe is from his collection. Bacon and chocolate, two of my favorite flavors—I had just never put them together. After eating a bowl of Jason's ice cream, they are now permanently wed in my mind.

3 to 5 slices uncooked thick-cut bacon
4 1/2 ounces quality milk chocolate
Flaky sea salt

1 recipe Homemade Vanilla Ice Cream (page 214)

Cut the bacon strips in half and place on a foil-lined cookie sheet and put into a cold oven.

Heat the oven to 400 degrees and cook the bacon until crisp, about 20 minutes. The more crisp, the better.

Drain the cooked bacon on a paper towel–lined plate and blot the top side with paper towels to remove excess grease.

In the top part of a double boiler, melt the milk chocolate over simmering water. Do not allow the water to touch the bottom of the top boiler or the chocolate will scorch.

Place the cooled bacon on waxed paper and using a pastry brush apply a thick coat of chocolate. Let the chocolate harden before turning the bacon over and applying another thick coat to the other side.

Lightly sprinkle flaky sea salt on each piece.

Allow the chocolate to continue to cool until firm. Place the bacon pieces in the freezer for about 12 hours prior to adding to the ice cream.

Remove chocolate-covered bacon from freezer and chop into bite-size pieces.

About 2 minutes prior to the end of the churning process, add the chopped bacon and resume churning.

Makes 2 quarts.

STRAWBERRY TORTE CAKE

This cake is a favorite of employees at Walton Communities. It was made for special employee gatherings by one of their coworkers, Barbara Brown. Before her death, Barbara shared the recipe with only one person other than her family—Lynda Ausburn. Lynda thinks it's the best cake ever, so she has gotten permission from Barbara's family to share it with us.

Cake
2 cups plus 2 tablespoons all-purpose
   flour
1 teaspoon baking soda
1 teaspoon baking powder
1/2 teaspoon salt
1 cup sugar
1/2 cup vegetable shortening
3 large eggs
1 1/2 teaspoons vanilla extract
1 1/2 teaspoons almond extract
1 cup whole milk
16 ounces strawberries, washed, leaves
   removed
1 (6- or 8-ounce) carton frozen, chopped
   strawberries in syrup, thawed but not
   drained
1 (16-ounce) carton whipped topping,
   thawed

Meringue
5 egg whites
1/2 cup sugar
1 cup pecans, chopped

Preheat the oven to 350 degrees. Grease and flour three 9-inch round cake pans.

To make the cake: In a medium bowl sift the flour, baking soda, baking powder, and salt together.

Place the sugar and shortening in the bowl of a stand mixer and cream until combined well. The sugar will seem to "melt" into the shortening and the mixture won't be at all granular.

Add the eggs, one at a time, mixing just until you can no longer see the egg. Scrape down the sides and the bottom after the last addition and lightly mix.

Add the vanilla and almond extracts to the milk.

Beginning and ending with the flour mixture, add one-third of the flour and half of the milk to the wet mixture until both are incorporated into the batter.

Scrape down the sides and the bottom and mix lightly, just enough to incorporate.*

Divide the batter among the 3 cake pans.

To make the meringue: Beat the egg whites in a medium bowl with a stand mixer until they are foamy. Gradually add the sugar and beat until the whites are stiff but not dry.

Spread one-third of the meringue on top of each unbaked cake layer.

Sprinkle the pecans on top of the meringue and bake the layers for 30 minutes. Meringues should be brown when the cake is done.

Leave the cakes in the pans for 10 to 15 minutes to cool before turning out onto a wire rack to cool completely.

Assembling the cake:

Cut about half of the fresh strawberries in half, setting them aside to place on top of the cake.

Slice the remaining strawberries and mix them in a large bowl with the thawed strawberries and juice.

Place the first cake layer meringue side up on a cake plate.

Spread a third of the whipped topping on top of the layer (not on the sides).

Top the whipped topping with half of the sliced strawberries and juice.

Place the second layer, meringue side up, on top of the strawberries and spread another third of the whipped topping on top of the second layer, followed by the remaining strawberries and their juices.

Place the third layer on top of the strawberries and spread the remaining whipped topping over the meringue.

Decorate the top of the cake with the fresh berries, cut side down.

Refrigerate until ready to serve. Refrigerate leftovers (if there are any).

Makes 14 to 16 servings.

* It's hard to over-beat a cake when you're creaming the butter and the sugar. However, once you begin adding the flour and the liquid, you want to mix just enough to incorporate the wet with the dry. At this point over-mixing will incorporate too much air into the batter and the cake will fall when it comes out of the oven.

CHERRY NUT CAKE

My Grandmother Howell always made every family member's favorite cake for their birthday. This was my sister Kay's choice. Mine was the German Chocolate that we make at Gabriel's using her recipe. One summer before I learned to write cursive I recopied her recipes into a black-and-white speckled composition notebook. I guess I've always loved good food and cookbooks! The cherries in the cake add such color and flavor, so I decided to combine those with my favorite yellow cake recipe. I know my assignment every year for my sister's birthday.

....

Cake
1 1/3 cups butter, softened
2 1/2 cups plus 2 tablespoons sugar
5 extra-large eggs, separated
3 cups cake flour, sifted before
    measuring
Heaping 1/2 teaspoon salt
2 1/2 teaspoons baking powder
1/4 cup maraschino cherry juice
1/4 teaspoon red food coloring, optional
1/2 cup milk
1 cup sour cream
1 teaspoon vanilla extract
1/2 cup maraschino cherries, drained and
    sliced fine
1/2 cup pecans, chopped

7-Minute Frosting
1 cup sugar
1/2 cup corn syrup
1/4 teaspoon cream of tartar
1/4 teaspoon salt
1 1/2 teaspoons vanilla extract
3 large egg whites
3 tablespoons water

....

To make the cake: Preheat the oven to 350 degrees. Grease and flour three 9-inch round cake pans.

Place the butter in the large bowl of a stand mixer and process on low speed. Gradually add the sugar and increase the speed to medium to thoroughly cream. After 3 to 4 minutes, scrape down the bottom and sides of the bowl. Continue beating on medium speed until the mixture is soft and fluffy.

Add the egg yolks, one at a time, beating just until combined.

Sift the flour, salt, and baking powder together in medium bowl.

In another medium bowl whisk together the cherry juice, food coloring, milk, sour cream, and vanilla.

Add one-third of the flour mixture to the creamed sugar and butter. Next, add one-half of the cherry juice mixture, continuing to add alternately the flour, then juice, ending with flour. Blend after each addition, just until no more flour is visible. Scrape down the bottom and sides of the bowl and lightly blend again.

Wash and dry the beaters before beating egg whites or use a hand mixer.

Begin beating the egg whites at medium speed. Increase to high and continue to beat until they will hold a soft peak.

Fold the cherries and pecans into the cake batter and then gently fold in the egg whites. Combine evenly but just until you can no longer see the whites.

Divide the batter evenly among the cake pans and bake for 35 to 40 minutes.

The layers are done when a cake tester inserted near the center comes out clean.

Leave the cakes in the pans about 10 minutes before turning out onto a wire rack to cool completely before frosting.

To make the frosting: Combine the sugar, corn syrup, cream of tartar, salt, vanilla, egg whites, and water into the top of a double boiler. Fill the bottom boiler half full of water and bring to a boil over medium-high heat. Place the top boiler over the boiling water and use a hand mixer to whip at a high speed for 7 or 8 minutes.

To assemble the cake: Place the first cake layer on a cake plate. Spread about one-fourth of the frosting on top. Place the second layer on top and spread another one-fourth of the frosting on top. Add the third layer on top and use the remaining frosting on the top and sides of the cake.

Makes 12 to 14 servings.

TIP: At Gabriel's we always whip for 8 minutes or so to be sure the frosting is thick enough to be a good spreading and holding consistency.

First Lady's Luncheon

An invitation to the First Lady's Luncheon in Washington, DC, was not on my radar. I visit the DC area on a regular basis because my oldest daughter, Stephanie, and her family live in northern Virginia. I've been to the monuments, seen the White House and the Mall at Christmas, toured the White House with Billie Gingrey, wife of Georgia congressman Phil Gingrey, walked under the blooming cherry trees, visited the Smithsonian, held my second grandson when he was only a few hours old, saw the smoke from the Pentagon on September 11th, welcomed my precious granddaughter from China to the U.S., sold goods at the Metropolitan Cooking Show, and been on stage there with Paula Deen.

The First Lady's Luncheon was another sort of adventure. Every moment of the two days were charged with excitement and anticipation! Billie Gingrey was the chairperson of the whole event. Billie worked tirelessly on the details for over a year, and seeing her hard work come to fruition was a privilege. She wanted to showcase Georgia talent, and I was overwhelmed that Gabriel's was included. At a gathering in Congressman Gingrey's office the evening before, I ate bread and butter pickles made by Janet Byington from Rome, Georgia, and promptly asked if she would share the recipe. It's on page 252 in this book. They are so good. At a reception prior to the luncheon, five hundred cheese straws baked by the folks at Gabriel's were served alongside Georgia pecans and mimosas.

Billie chose the theme of "Patriotism from the Front Porch" for the event. Georgia artist Steve Penley, internationally known for his unique style of bold color, strong brush strokes, and vivid imagery was commissioned to do a painting to honor Mrs. Obama for her work with military families. All who attended were gifted with a print of Mr. Penley's artwork as well as a print of Georgia's own Howard Finster's "The Fish of the Sea." Mr. Finster is a self-taught artist and is known as "The Grandfather of Southern Folk Art."

Georgia's own warm and charming First Lady, Sandra Deal, wife of our governor Nathan Deal, was there. Paula Deen, cousin, and another "first" on my list of special people, was present. Paula, in collaboration with Executive Chef Andre Coté of the Washington Hilton Hotel, planned the menu for the event.

Dishes with a definite Southern flair were served to the 1,500 attendees. I rarely sit down for more than five minutes to eat lunch, but I wasn't going to miss a bite of the Quinoa Hoppin' John Terrine with Baby Greens and Bacon, Paula Deen's Sweet Georgia Peach Honey Shrimp on Sweet Pea Puree with Sweet Potato Risotto, and Chef Andre's "Front Porch" Pecan Sticky Toffee Pudding with Peach Ice Cream. I cleaned my plate, of course.

The highlight of the luncheon was the arrival of Mrs. Obama, the official First Lady. She is strikingly beautiful, gracious, and seemed down to earth. She smiled a lot and appeared to thoroughly enjoy the event. Mrs. Obama spoke from her heart suggesting that all Americans have an ability and duty to contribute to Americans in various stages of need and hurt. She expressed faith that Americans will successfully handle the social and physical challenges facing our ever-changing America. She was inspiring.

After lunch we were entertained by Trisha Yearwood, a Monticello, Georgia, native, a great country music singer, wife of Garth Brooks, author of a best-selling cookbook and host to a cooking show, *Trisha's Southern Kitchen*. She made us Georgians proud, and I was thrilled to have my picture taken with Trisha and Paula.

There were many photo ops during those two days, new friendships were made, and old ones enjoyed. It was an adventure this Georgia cook never thought she would have. And looking back down the road I am so grateful for the many opportunities that have come my way.

PECAN PRALINES

One my greatest temptations when I visit Savannah or attend a wedding that is catered by Lee Epting from Athens is to make a glutton of myself on their pralines, another Southern culinary icon. While in Washington, DC, for the 101st First Lady's Luncheon, I attended a reception at Congressman Gingrey's office. I immediately spotted the pecan pralines and proceeded to find out from whence they came. They were made by Janet Byington of Rome, Georgia, whom I had gotten to know. This is her mother's recipe, and she agreed to share it with all of us. Make these delicious pralines and who knows what great invitation you might get.

1 (16-ounce) box dark brown sugar
2 cups white sugar
1 cup whipping cream
1/2 cup milk

3 tablespoons butter
2 cups pecan halves, chopped (not too small)

Combine the brown sugar and white sugar in a heavy medium saucepan. Whisk in the cream and milk and blend well.

Cook over medium heat bringing to a boil and cook to slightly above the soft boil stage (about 240 to 245 degrees on an instant-read thermometer).

Remove from heat and add the butter. Beat by hand with a wooden spoon about 2 minutes until the mixture is smooth and creamy and it begins to lose its gloss. Be careful not to beat too long or it will harden too soon.

Add nuts and drop by the spoonful onto waxed paper.

Let cool. Store in an airtight container.

Makes about 50 pralines.

PECAN PIE

This pie is truly a Southern classic. I've eaten many pieces of pecan pie, but my favorite recipe is the one we bake at Gabriel's. It's simple and delicious. Pecan pie is another example of folks taking a native product and turning it into a delicious legend.

1 cup sugar
2 cups corn syrup
1/2 cup (1 stick) butter, softened
6 large eggs

1 teaspoon vanilla extract
2 unbaked 9-inch deep-dish piecrusts*
3 cups pecan pieces or halves

Preheat the oven to 325 degrees.

In a large bowl combine the sugar, corn syrup, butter, eggs, and vanilla. Beat or whisk just long enough to combine well.

Place the unbaked piecrusts on a cookie sheet.

Divide the pecans between the two piecrusts. Pour the liquid over the pecans. The crusts will be very full.

Bake the pies for 40 to 45 minutes or until the filling is set and golden. The center may be slightly soft, but if it's loose add a little more cooking time.

Set the pies on a wire rack to cool. Serve warm with vanilla ice cream or standing alone at room temperature.

Makes 2 pies or 12 to 16 servings.

PLAYING IN THE KITCHEN: Add 1/4 to 1/3 cup semisweet chocolate chips when you add the pecans. You will have a little filling left over. Or drizzle with store-bought caramel sauce, chocolate sauce, or melted white chocolate chips.

* A store-bought piecrust can be used, but if time permits make a homemade crust. See recipe on page 193.

THIS AND THAT

Mulled Cider

Mulled Wine

Minted Peach Lemonade

Crème Fraîche

Chimichurri Sauce

Avocado Mayonnaise

Slow Cooker Apple Butter

Cranberry Aioli

Barbecue Sauce

Caramelized Nuts

Bread and Butter Pickles

MULLED CIDER

My friend Sally Rhoden serves this drink at her annual Christmas caroling party. This cider is a big hit with young and old on a cold evening.

2 1/4 cups sugar
3 quarts water, divided
1/4 teaspoon cloves
1/4 teaspoon ginger
3 sticks cinnamon

6 tablespoons freshly squeezed lemon juice
2 (6-ounce) small cans frozen orange juice concentrate, thawed
1/2 gallon apple cider

Combine the sugar and 1 quart of water in a large saucepan. Bring to a boil over high heat and simmer for 10 minutes. Remove the pan from the heat and whisk in the cloves, ginger, and cinnamon and let stand for 1 hour. Add the lemon juice, orange juice concentrate, cider, and the remaining 2 quarts of water. Return to the stove and warm over medium-low heat, but do not boil. Pour into individual mugs and serve hot.

Makes 28 to 32 (6-ounce) servings.

NOTE: Add a jigger of Amaretto to the mug of cider for an adult version.

MULLED WINE

This mulled wine is an adult treat for my friend Sally Rhoden's Christmas caroling group. Even more warming than her mulled cider and wine is the joy Sally brings to her guests when she plays her guitar and leads us in singing favorite hymns and popular tunes.

1 cup sugar
1/2 cup water
2 sticks cinnamon
2 1/2 lemons, sliced

2 dozen cloves
4 cups orange juice
1 quart red wine (claret, burgundy, etc.)

Mix the sugar, water, cinnamon sticks, lemons, and cloves in a large saucepan. Bring to a boil over high heat. Allow to boil until the mixture becomes syrupy. Strain the syrup into another large container. Pour the syrup back into saucepan and add the juice and wine and warm over low heat, but do not boil. Serve hot.

Makes 8 to 10 servings.

1

2

3

4

Hospitality in a glass

5

6

7

8

MINTED PEACH LEMONADE

Great over crushed ice for a luncheon on a hot summer day, a Sunday supper, or a concert in the park.

2 cups loosely packed fresh mint leaves
1 1/3 cups sugar
2 cups freshly squeezed lemon juice
   (8 to 12 lemons)

6 cups cold water
1 cup canned peach nectar, chilled
Thinly sliced lemons, optional

In a large bowl or pitcher, muddle the mint leaves and sugar with the back of a spoon. Add the lemon juice and water and stir until the sugar dissolves. Add the peach nectar and stir. Strain into a serving pitcher. Drop in a few thinly sliced lemons for color. Serve over ice.

Makes 10 to 12 servings.

Minted Peach Lemonade (page 239)

CRÈME FRAÎCHE

Crème fraîche isn't often thought of as Southern, but it's delicious as an addition to many things. If you're lucky enough to have the opportunity to enjoy caviar, it's absolutely essential. Crème fraîche can be used on pasta and vegetables, in sauces, or as a topping for desserts. Keep some on hand and when you're feeling creative, try it.

1 cup heavy cream
2 tablespoons buttermilk

In a small bowl combine the heavy cream and the buttermilk. Cover and let sit on the counter for 8 to 16 hours. It will thicken up but still be pourable. Store in the refrigerator up to 1 week.

If serving with caviar, you'll also need finely chopped red onion, hard-boiled eggs, drained capers, and toast points.

Makes 1 cup.

CHIMICHURRI SAUCE

This is a much-used condiment in Latin and South America. I love this fresh and light sauce with fish, grilled meats, or fresh vegetables. Make it in the food processor or hand chop it for a more chunky sauce. Ed Gabriel shared his version with me.

1/2 cup packed fresh cilantro
1/2 cup extra-virgin olive oil
1 cup fresh Italian flat-leaf parsley
1 tablespoon minced garlic
1/4 cup lemon juice

1/2 teaspoon cumin
1/2 teaspoon salt
1/2 teaspoon red pepper flakes
2 tablespoons minced shallots

Combine the cilantro, olive oil, parsley, garlic, lemon juice, cumin, salt, red pepper flakes, and shallots in the bowl of a food processor and puree until smooth. Refrigerate for up to 2 weeks.

Makes 1 to 1 1/2 cups.

Avocado Mayonnaise

Avocadoes are full of vitamins A and K. Add this mayonnaise to your next turkey or chicken sandwich, burger, egg salad, or deviled eggs.

1 ripe avocado
2 cups mayonnaise

Dash of fresh lemon juice

Peel the avocado and remove the seed. Mash it in a medium bowl. Add the mayonnaise and lemon juice and stir to combine well. Refrigerate for up to 4 days.

Makes 2 1/2 cups.

A biscuit's
best friend

SLOW COOKER APPLE BUTTER

Shawn, one of Sally Rhoden's grandsons, loves this dish. It's perfect on biscuits or toast.

8 tart apples, peeled, cored, and sliced
2 teaspoons ground cinnamon

$^1/_2$ teaspoon ground nutmeg
2 cups sugar

Combine the apples, cinnamon, nutmeg, and sugar in a large slow cooker and cook on high for 2 hours. Turn to low and cook for 18 hours. Remove from the slow cooker and let cool. Store in the refrigerator until ready to use. Will keep up to one week in the refrigerator.

Makes 6 to 8 cups.

Slow Cooker Apple Butter (page 245)

CRANBERRY AIOLI

Mayonnaise is the base for an "aioli." So many of your favorite flavors and ingredients can be combined with the mayo to yield great condiments. Use this on those leftover Thanksgiving turkey sandwiches or roasted chicken sandwiches all year long.

1/2 cup cranberry sauce
3 heaping tablespoons mayonnaise

1/2 teaspoon dried rosemary

Place the cranberry sauce, mayonnaise, and dried rosemary in a small bowl and whisk until smooth. Store in the refrigerator up to 7 days.

Makes 1/4 to 1/2 cup.

BARBECUE SAUCE

Meredith Dykes shared this family recipe with me. We now use it in our Brunswick stew and on our barbecue pork sandwiches. My Aunt Mabel Bass of Albany, Georgia, cooked barbecue and stew nearly every Friday night during the summer and had the whole family over. This sauce reminds me of the summer weeks I spent there with her and Grandmother and Granddaddy Heath.

1/4 cup (1/2 stick) butter, melted
1 3/4 cups ketchup
1/4 cup firmly packed brown sugar
1/4 cup prepared mustard
1/4 cup white vinegar
2 tablespoons Worcestershire sauce

1 to 2 tablespoons hot sauce
1 tablespoon liquid smoke
1 1/2 teaspoons lemon juice
1 1/2 teaspoons minced garlic
1 teaspoon coarsely ground black pepper
1/2 teaspoon crushed red pepper

In a heavy saucepan over low heat, combine the butter, ketchup, brown sugar, mustard, vinegar, Worcestershire, hot sauce, liquid smoke, lemon juice, garlic, black pepper, and red pepper. Cook for 25 to 30 minutes, stirring often. Store in the refrigerator for up to 10 days.

Makes 1 1/2 cups.

CARAMELIZED NUTS

These are on our Pumpkin Praline Pie and Baby Blue Salad. Always delicious on almost any salad or dessert.

1 cup pecans
1/2 cup brown sugar

4 tablespoons butter

In a skillet over medium heat, add the pecans, brown sugar, and butter. Stir until the sugar has melted and the pecans are coated and sticky. After cooling completely, store in an airtight container up to two weeks.

Makes 1 cup.

BREAD AND BUTTER PICKLES

When I attended a reception the evening before the First Lady's Luncheon in Washington, DC, I had the pleasure of sampling these pickles made by Janet Byington. When I mentioned that I was writing this cookbook, she told me she came from a long line of good Southern cooks. I asked her to share some of her best recipes with me. The following is her family recipe.

6 pounds firm cucumbers, sliced into $^1/4$-inch slices
2 green bell peppers with seeds removed, sliced into $^1/4$-inch rings
8 small white onions, skins removed and sliced (1 $^1/2$ to 1 $^3/4$ pounds)
$^1/2$ cup salt

1 quart crushed ice
5 cups distilled white vinegar
5 cups sugar
3 teaspoons turmeric
1 teaspoon ground cloves
4 teaspoons mustard seeds
2 teaspoons celery seeds

Layer the sliced cucumbers, bell peppers, and onions in a large bowl. Sprinkle with the salt and cover with 1 quart or more of crushed ice.

Cover with a weighted lid and place in the refrigerator for 3 hours.

In a 12-quart stockpot combine the vinegar and sugar, stirring well to blend. Add the turmeric, cloves, mustard seeds, and celery seeds, and stir well. Set in the refrigerator until the vegetables have chilled for 3 hours.

After 3 hours in the refrigerator, drain the vegetables and add to the stockpot. Heat the pot over low heat with very little stirring and bring them to just below the boiling point.

Prepare the jars, rings, and lids according to manufacturer's directions, or place them in the dishwasher with no other dishes and run through the wash/rinse cycle. Don't use any jars that are chipped or lids or rings that are rusted.

Fill the hot jars with hot cucumbers. Ladle the hot liquid over the cucumbers, covering them completely, leaving about $^1/2$-inch headspace.

Insert a knife down the side of the jar and go around the jar removing any air bubbles. With a clean, hot cloth wash off any liquid you may have spilled on the jar. Place the lids and rings on the jars. Tighten the ring.

Process the jars for 10 minutes in a boiling-water bath.

Remove the jars from the water bath and set on the counter to cool. Tighten any rings that may have loosened. You will hear little pings as the lids seal. Allow to cool completely. Any lids that do not seal should be refrigerated and used within a few days.

Store in a cool, dry place until ready to use. Refrigerate a jar for several hours before serving and refrigerate any unused, opened jar of pickles.

Makes 8 pints.

NOTE: Many people who pickle and preserve a lot would probably not put these pickles through a water bath. Being in the food business I am often overly cautious. I heard my jars "pinging," meaning they were sealing themselves, as they were sitting on the table waiting for their water bath. My advice is to read a bit on canning and then follow the procedure with which you are comfortable.

My water bath didn't require any special equipment because this is really a small quantity to process. I made the pots I had work by using the same 12-quart stockpot that I had made my syrup in (after washing, of course) for the water bath. I took the metal insert from a large steamer that happened to fit into my stockpot to set my jars in and then lowered them into the water bath in the stockpot. I made sure the water covered the jars by 1 inch and brought the water back up to a boil and simmered the jars for 10 minutes. After removing from the water, I let them sit on the counter to cool before storing them in a cool, dry place.

For those who want to pursue canning and preserving, a water bath canner can be purchased very reasonably at most large discount stores or online. It's really a lot of fun to stash away fresh fruits and vegetables for later use. You'll feel so productive!

ACKNOWLEDGMENTS

This book has come together via the hands and minds of many good folks. Once again, Heather Skelton, my editor with Thomas Nelson, has guided me all the way through our second book together. She is well acquainted with the demands that my restaurant and bakery, Gabriel's, puts on my life. During a project such as this, she works around me, cajoles me, and sometimes uses the cattle prod. I appreciate her expertise in writing, knowledge of food and preparation, and her talent for organization.

This is also the second book that friend and chef Debbie Willyard has done with me. I call her friend because she is ever ready, willing, and joyful about us working and playing together. I call her "chef" because she is a chef and loves to channel her energy, talent, and creativity into preparing delicious food, along with being a wife and mom. Debbie worked with me on the photo shoot for *Second Helpings* and still volunteered her home and talent for five days of the shoot for this book. What a challenge she had balancing home life, a kitchen full of food and pots and pans, a photographer who was very soon to be a new mom, a food stylist, an anxious editor, and a harried writer and restaurant/bakery owner. Coinciding with the writing of this cookbook, Gabriel's also opened its first kiosk at Atlanta's Hartsfield Airport. Through the gifts of love and patience, we are still friends!

The photography and food styling team of photographer Stephanie Mullins and food stylist Teresa Blackburn rounded out our foursome for the photo shoot. I had not worked with the two of them before but I am thrilled with the beautiful shots that we have as a result of their talent and hard work.

Of course, there would be no need for an editor or a photo shoot without recipes. When I think of Southern food, as with all other cultures, I think of recipes that have been handed down from grandmothers and mothers to daughters and sons. That is exactly the collection we have in this book. I am very grateful to the friends and family who opened their family's history of good food and shared the family favorites with me. You will see their names as you read through and cook from this book. I hope you will be able to sense the warmth and love that the sharing of good food helps to weave into the fabric of your family.

I have collected recipes all my life. I remember copying my Grandmother Howell's recipes into a composition notebook for her during the summer. Other family recipes I know just from cooking and spending time in the kitchen with my mother, grandmothers, and aunt. Some of them have never been written down until now. I have a wealth of information from my beloved restaurant, and due to a faithful staff, I am able to share some of them in this book.

The proofing of a book is not just the checking of spelling. We have the gift of "spell check" to nag us as we write. But true proofing requires the gift of knowledge of cooking and the flow of recipes. Heather Skelton, editor extraordinaire, along with Sally Rhoden, Cindy Dye, Robin Anderson, and Ginny McNabb, performed "virtual" preparation as we proofed this book.

A project such as this doesn't come together without the love and encouragement of family and friends. Recipes must be tested and the willing hands and hearts of Sally Rhoden and Emily Teddy are a treasure to me. Sally Rhoden, who has raised her children and she continues to play an active role in the lives of her children and seven grandchildren as well as contributing mightily in our community, found time to cook and test. Emily Teddy, a precious new friend, young wife, and mother, is a natural in the kitchen. She worked side-by-side in the kitchen with me and at her own home to confirm the goodness of some of the recipes I'm sharing with you.

We are amply endowed with professionals at Gabriel's, such as Jeffry Webb,

Beth Granato, and Jennifer Dauphin, who shared their expertise with me. My coworkers: ever faithful, "sister," Pam Addicks, along with Mo Bednarowski, Susan Hutcheson, Denver Woods, and Renee Bastain, held down the storefront so that I could write and cook.

The sales team at Thomas Nelson always works hard for me to get the word out that I have a new book. It's a privilege to have them represent my efforts.

Paula Deen has once again written my foreword. What a joy it is for me to have the "First Lady" of Southern cuisine speak about my books. More than write words about me, over the years she has spoken words of encouragement to me. She is another one of the women in my family who model love of people, hard work, and never giving up.

It brings such joy to my life to be surrounded and nurtured by such a group of people as these. I hope that through the efforts and talents of these folks, you find recipes that become your family's favorites and you experience the joy of cooking.

ABOUT THE AUTHOR

Johnnie Gabriel started baking cakes alongside her grandmother as a young girl in South Georgia.

Today, Johnnie is known as Atlanta's "Cake Lady" for her mouth-watering red velvet cupcakes, award-winning wedding cakes, and other delectable desserts.

Johnnie's restaurant and bakery, Gabriel's, serves homemade Southern comfort food for breakfast, lunch, and dinner. On any given day, you're likely to see Johnnie greeting customers and serving up fresh veggies, cornbread, and sweet tea.

Johnnie lives in Marietta, Georgia, surrounded by friends and family who continue to support her along life's journey.

Cooking with the grandkids: Laney, Heath, and Wyatt

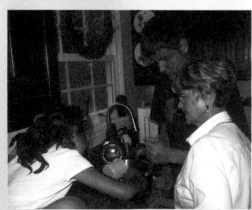

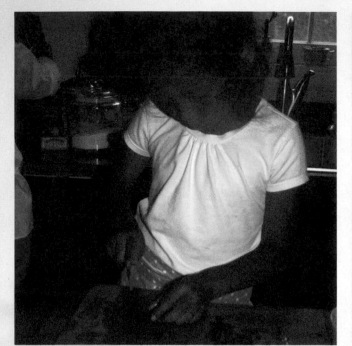

INDEX